The Education of the Women of India

The Education of the Women of India

MINNA G COWAN, M.A. (T.C.D.)

GYAN

Published by

Gyan Publishing House
5, Ansari Road
Daryaganj, New Delhi-110002
Phone: 011-47034999, 9811692060
E-mail: books@gyanbooks.com

Distribution Network
gyanbooks.com
India, USA, Canada, UK, Australia, France

ISBN : 978-81-212-9222-1 (PB)
First Published, 1912

2nd Impression 2023

Printed at: Gyan Press, Delhi.

The Education of the Women of India
Author: MINNA G COWAN

A Parsi Girl

The Education of the Women of India

By

MINNA G COWAN, M.A. (T.C.D.)

Girton College

ILLUSTRATED

Fleming H. Revell Company

New York Chicago Toronto

Preface

It has been well said that no Western should attempt to make any general statement about inscrutable India ; the most he can venture to say is, that "in certain places certain things which he saw may possibly have been what he thought they really were." The present volume is therefore based upon appearances which may or may not have represented reality, upon conversations with Government officials, missionaries and Indian friends, who kindly gave of their leisure to a stranger, and upon the study of Government Reports. Where any generalization has been made, the writer trusts it will be taken with the reservations which a very brief residence in the East renders needful. If the book help the women of the West to realize how critical is the present evolutionary period in the education of the women of India, especially in its relation to constructive Christianity, it will not have failed of its purpose.

My thanks are specially due to Miss Richardson and Miss M'Dougall of Westfield College for aid in revision, to many friends for their unstinted help, and to the Faculty of Advocates for the use of their Library. M. G. C.

EDINBURGH, *July* 1912.

To

the

G. A.

Contents

Illustrations

Statistical Tables

APPENDIX

I

INTRODUCTION

> "That is true knowledge which can make
> Us mortals saintlike, holy, pure,
> The strange thirst of the spirit slake
> And strengthen suffering to endure."
>
> TORU DUTT.

TO write a book on the education of Indian women is a prosaic action impelled by Western devotion to matter of fact; it would be more fitting to write of the veil of mystic romance which has hidden the sorrows and the joys of Indian women from the world; of the Rajput women who issued from the royal zenana to lead a forlorn cause against their country's foes, or passed by hundreds to a fiery death rather than touch the conqueror's hand; of those whose intrigue and strategy were redeemed from falseness by underlying devotion to others, of those who rose above the symbols of ritual and worship to the true perception of the Divine in life. But the modern world of the East has its own romance, that of the meeting of diverse civilizations, of the craving for truth and reality, of multitudes in the valley of decision. The old chivalry is there in a new form. It is not a little thing to open the door of self-realization, with its opportunity for an even greater selflessness, to the myriads of Indian women. The new thought and new ideals which are permeating the whole East have no more striking phase than their manifestation in the life of women. The tentative attitude towards growing freedom, the hesitation to enter in and possess, the recurring tragedy of those who are ahead of their times, and of others for whom the new wine is too strong, are only partial aspects of a problem which cuts deep into modern civilization. The women who live behind the veil in India, or who, though without, are utterly untouched by modern education and modern ideas, are still the vast majority, and there is in no sense a Feminist movement such as exists in Japan and to a certain extent in China; still, the new type is there, the pioneer in a transitional period and the fruit of modern education. A Mohammedan lady of good social standing in Bombay keeps a school for poor girls in her own house, and has completely given up *parda*; Brāhma Samāj [1] ladies are doing excellent work on Government Education Committees; an orthodox Hindu lady goes on tour to advocate a special system of Hindu schools; an Ārya

[1] An Indian Theistic sect eclectic in character, founded by Raja Rammohan Roy in Calcutta, 1828. *Cp. New Ideas in India*—John Morrison, D.D.

Samāj[2] widow staffs a school for high caste girls in her own house with entirely voluntary teachers. An excellent Ladies' Magazine is edited by an Indian woman graduate in Madras. A Parsi woman holds the position of Legal Adviser for *parda-nashin*[3] women to the Government of Bengal. Indian women are found doing excellent work as doctors, and a few as principals of girls' schools. It would be easy to multiply examples not only of those who have taken up definite professional life, but also of others who share in the work and interests of their husbands as closely as any woman of the West, and who use their social influence on the side of progress; the Maharani of Baroda has written a book to interpret to her more secluded countrywomen the many phases of the Englishwoman's life; the Begum of Bhopal, on her return from the Coronation, summoned the Ladies' Club of her capital to exhort them once more on the never-failing theme of education as the root of all progress; the Rani of Gondal and many other Indian princesses take a personal interest in the welfare of their people. The same phase is also to be seen in other ranks; we find the orthodox Hindu wife of an Indian Deputy Commissioner accompanying him on tour through his district, rather than that he should live the

[2] Or Vedic Theistic Association, a patriotic and religious sect, chiefly in the United Provinces and the Punjāb. Founded in 1875 by Dyanand Saraswati. *Cp.* as above.

Women who remain behind the curtain.

greater part of his life apart from her.[4] Then there are the transitional types, women who venture thus far and tremble on the brink of many complicated problems; the wives of "England-returned" men, whose anglicized husbands have done their best to educate them, and by leading them painfully through the new ideas to bring them, to some extent at least, into the "reformed life."[5] There is much that is pathetic here, and the tragedy of "The Broken Road," has its counterpart to-day in the heart of many an Indian girl, who knows that the husband who is studying in Britain will, when he returns, have entered a new world in which she can never share. And so by many stages one passes back to the old, the real, India, where the woman graduates in suffering, and where the babies seem to grow, with no stage of girlhood, into little women on whom the burden of life falls heavily. Yet who can say whether the influence of these "secluded ones" is not even yet the most potent factor in modern India?

The "advanced ones" have their corporate life, and one of the most interesting features in India to-day is the number of women's societies which are springing up, partly in conjunction with European ladies and partly by entirely spontaneous effort. The traveller accustomed to read of secluded Indian ladies would be surprised

[4] *Among Indian Rajahs and Ryots* — Sir Andrew H. L. Fraser, K.C.S.I.

[5] *Between the Twilights*—Cornelia Sorabji.

to visit the Princess Mary Victoria Gymkhana in Bombay and meet Parsi, Mohammedan and Hindu women playing croquet and Badminton, or having tea with their friends, and even entertaining men of their acquaintance twice a year. It is true that Parsi influence marks off the social life of Bombay from that of more conservative India, but the Bombay women do not always remain in Bombay. Some of the societies are linked with the various religious movements, others are purely social and educational. One society, the *Bharat Stri Mahamandal*, in the United Provinces and in Bengal, has been founded by Hindu and Moslem women, but is intended to include all sympathizers. Its aim is " to form a common centre for all women thinkers and co-workers of every race, creed, class, and party in India to associate themselves together for the progress of humanity." [6] Another, the *Gujerati Stri Mandal*, in Bombay, is a purely Hindu society, which aims at bringing many of the Gujerati women, who keep *parda*, into contact with other women, and has a definite if somewhat ambitious educational programme. *The Seva Sadan*, or Sisters Ministrant, a society established in Bombay in 1909, with four branches, is under a united committee of Hindu, Mohammedan, and Parsi representatives, and aims at philanthropic and educational work. " In the name of Him, Who has given us so many bene-

[6] *Women in the Modern National Movements of the East* (S.C.M. Pamphlet), by A. de Sélincourt.

dictions, we call upon every woman to become a Benediction, and we call upon all who realize that India's two great sins are her sin against women and her sin against the depressed, to help us in creating Sisters Ministrant." [7] The vow which these Sisters Ministrant are called upon to take, is to "look upon life as a sacred trust for loving, self-sacrificing service, and to do such service. So help me God." It is true that when the high idealism of this prospectus and report are compared with actual fact, there is evident a certain lack of reality, characteristic of many Indian schemes. Still, good work, not unlike that of a London Settlement, is being actually done by two splendid women at the society's Settlement in Bombay, and idealism never fails of its ultimate fruit.

No account of the corporate life of Indian women would be complete without mention of the National Indian Association, which, though organized from London, has many Indian ladies as secretaries or committee members of its Ladies' Branches in India. Amongst its many activities one of the most effective has been the holding of *parda* lectures and other gatherings for the encouragement of education, and scholarships are also awarded through it to suitable candidates. Apart from all organization, the *parda* party, pure and simple, whether given by the wives of Government officials, or by private individuals, has its own part to play. The honour of holding

Seva Sadan Report.

the first of these, as a species of feminine *durbar*, belongs probably to Lady Amherst.[8] At the request of the famous Baiza Pai, wife of the Maharaj of Scindhia, she received a deputation of Maratha ladies at Agra in 1827, and the account translated from a Persian letter by one of the guests reveals the quaint misconception of all things Western under which the deputation laboured. The number of Lord Amherst's supposed wives, the English "nautch girls," who played the table with the ivory teeth, the strange attitude of the English ladies, reveal a world far apart, and though the modern *parda* party may not be needed to-day to dispel such extreme delusions, it is still a meeting ground for worlds far apart, and the source of many new ideas to both English and Indian ladies. These gatherings and societies have an extraordinary influence especially on those who have fought shy of the proffered friendship of the missionaries, or of Government educational effort, and they certainly count for much in the breaking down of artificial barriers to progress.

The "secluded ones" of the real India have no corporate life and belong to no society save that of the family. The unit of Indian civilization is the family, and where that word includes the joint-family to remote degrees, one may perhaps faintly understand what the corporate influence of the women of the household means, and measure it against the impotence of a mere society.

[8] *Ruler of India Series*—Lord Amherst.

Such in all its variety is the diverse life of the women of India to-day, the meeting-place of two civilizations, and fraught with untold consequences and influences for the future. Hitherto the weight of woman's opinion has been conservative and religious. "A combination of enforced ignorance and overdone religion have not only made women in India willing victims of customs unjust and hurtful in the highest degree, but it has also made them the most formidable because the most effective opponents of all change or innovation."[9] But signs have not been wanting to show that this same influence has been inflammatory of revolution and sedition, and instances are given, by a recent writer, of ladies' meetings in which sympathy was extended even to anarchists who had been guilty of murder, and in which ladies gathered together in zenanas were urged to do all they could to advance a mischievous propaganda.[10] True, this kind of influence is not widespread, but it is a natural result when impressionable characters are brought into contact with ideas which they have not the knowledge nor opportunity of weighing aright. There is the farther risk of recoil from enforced restraint towards the liberty which is not a law unto itself. The slavish imitation of the West which has marred much of the modern movement in the

[9] Speech at the Education Congress, 1897—G. K. Gokhale.

[10] *Among Indian Rajahs and Ryots*—Sir A. H. L. Fraser, K.C.S.I.

past and from which the Swadeshi of to-day is a reaction, is even more repellent in the life of women than of men, and the Indian world would lose much of its fascination and charm if instead of a rehabilitation of the ancient ideals of womanhood the modern type were to develop merely as a denationalized caricature. The classic Indian ideal of womanhood, with its wonderful vicarious suffering, its selflessness and devotion, is enough to make the world weep, yet it may be that it has proved throughout the centuries one of the subtlest temptations to the strong. "It is a terrible thing," writes Sister Nivedita, who made the Hindu woman's life her own; "it dwarfs the wife. I often think that it would be good for the husbands themselves if their wives were less soft and good." But the glory and the grace of it may live, and its gentle womanliness transfigure modern life. The Indian woman need lose none of those qualities which made her loved in Vedic times, but may prove to the world that she is conscious of her own heritage and capable of choosing only what is good from the life of the West.

History is made quietly, and the modern movement for the education of the women of India and its guidance along right lines is a matter of Imperial importance. On education of some sort they will insist. The latest Quinquennial Report (1907) shows an increase in the period of over 45 per cent. of the total number of girls at school, and since then some districts show even more.[11] The emphasis at present laid on girls' schools is in part the result of the general educational ferment in India. One hundred years have elapsed since Lord Minto wrote his famous letter to the Directors of the East India Company, animadverting on the decay of Hindu and Mohammedan science and learning; this letter was followed two years later by the decision to spend a lac of rupees anually for educational purposes, a paltry sum in comparison with the Government's educational outlay to-day, yet representing the inauguration of a new policy. The great principles of the systematic introduction of Western learning, with the English language as a medium of instruction in the higher stages; of the possession of English education as the criterion for Government service; of the direct responsibility of the State for secular instruction only, together with the encouragement of voluntary effort on other lines by a policy of grants-in-aid, have borne fruit far beyond the imagination of those who laid them down in the early half of last century. A vast system has grown up: five Universities with magnificent Government and missionary colleges, a network of Primary and Secondary schools both in British territory and the Native States, an Educational Department in every province under a Director of Public Instruction, centralized till recently under a Director-General, an expenditure in 1907 of public funds amounting to 559 lacs, and,

[11] *Cp.* Diagram, Appendix C.

along with all this, to-day, a grave criticism, representing various shades of political and religious opinion, of the work done, with a questioning of its beneficial influence and of the fundamental principles involved. Good results there certainly have been, but there is a tendency to-day to emphasize the weak points in the system rather than to lay stress on the actual good done, as always happens in a world bent on reform. The main points of the indictment brought against the system by current journalism are briefly these: an educated minority has been created, while only 28.7 per cent. of the present generation of boys are at school; the ranks of the lower Government services are overcrowded, and disappointed candidates turn only too readily to sedition; the Code tends to an abnormal development of the repetitive faculty; intellect is emphasized at the expense of character; the whole tendency is to take away from the Indian child his own historical heritage of thought and feeling. The Government is now devoting careful attention to the whole problem in its relation to the general political situation. In January 1911, a new Central Department of Education was formed, with a representative on the Governor-General's Council. Under its auspices a special Conference of the higher educational officials and others was recently held at Allahabad to discuss outlines of future policy, with special emphasis on the burning topics of Primary education and moral teaching. Lord

Hardinge personally visited incognito some of the students' "Messes"[12] in Calcutta to see the facts with his own eyes. The boon granted at the Durbar includes an additional expenditure of fifty lacs of rupees for educational purposes.

Apart from Government there is an expression in Indian circles of the sense of crisis, and of the need for the extension of popular education. Though doubtless engineered by a minority, still it is not without value. The Indian National Congress and the All-Indian Moslem League have passed resolutions in favour of compulsory Primary education which show some sense of what education really means. "Its universal diffusion is a matter of primary importance, for literacy is better than illiteracy; education is something more than the mere capacity to read and write. It means a keener enjoyment of life and a more refined standard of living. It means the greater moral and economic efficiency of the individual." In March 1911, Mr Gokhale introduced his Bill for Compulsory Primary Education to the Governor-General's Council, and thereby awakened discussion throughout the country. Idealistic it certainly is, when the dearth of trained teachers is considered and the conservatism of the real India taken into account, but it marks the trend of a certain section of Indian opinion. There is, moreover, a movement on the part of others for the establishment of Mohammedan and Hindu Universities, as a

[12] Lodgings.

reaction from the secularism of the Government institutions.

It is not the purpose of this book to analyse such criticism but merely to show its relation to the problem of women's education. To some thinkers the most fundamental flaw in the whole system has seemed the development of one-half of the community far beyond that of the other. In spite of recent progress the literate percentage is 10.50 for men, and only 10.4 for women;[13] the removal of this discrepancy might mean the raising of the whole of social life and go far towards the solution of other problems. Hence in every district there are ardent advocates of female education. "A realization of the necessity for an educated and emancipated womanhood is now no longer confined to those sections of the community which are directly influenced by Christianity, but is laying hold of Eastern nations as a whole."[14] Hardly a Congress or debating society exists which does not pass resolutions thereon, hardly an Indian journal which does not emphasize the importance of the feminine factor. "Upon the condition of women depends the happiness and prosperity of the homes. Upon their fitness will hinge the evolution of our character. The schools and universities may make us highly intellectual, but as for character

[13] 1911 Census Returns. In 1901, 9.8 per cent. men, 0.07 per cent. women.

[14] *Women in the Modern National Movements of the East* (S.C.M. Pamphlet, 1912), A. de Sélincourt.

we must look to the home and the home alone. Let us frankly say to the Indian girl: 'Here, child of God, take this key to the portals of knowledge: it belongs to you by right of birth. Enter then fearlessly and behold the beauty and the joys it reveals.' "[15] There is nothing more striking than the emphasis which is laid in these articles on the sanction found in the Vedic classics for the education of women and on the modern movement as a renaissance, and not an overthrow of ancient Aryan ideas. The Mohammedan case is a more difficult one to prove, but there are writers, such as Ameer Ali, strongly influenced by the Christian ideas of the West, who attempt it in spite of the Koran.[16] There is the even bolder spirit of those who hold that "though all the sacred *mantras* [17] were against it," the education of her women is the only solution of India's problem. The slow infiltration of the Christian ideal of woman has had its effect and the influence of missionary educational work has gained an increased momentum by the change in the Indian attitude. True, the conservative influence is still there with much of the old strength, as will be indicated in succeeding chapters, not only amongst the orthodox but amongst the more advanced. An Indian Reform Journal can still

[15] *Vedic Quarterly*, 1911.

[16] *Koran Sura IV*. (Rodwell's edition, *Sura*, C.).

[17] A secret phrase or password used for initiation into Hindu sects. *Cp. Primer of Hinduism*—J. N. Farquhar (C.L.S.).

publish an advertisement of an undergraduate who desires a wife of eleven years, educated in Hindi and domestic matters. Such are the strange anomalies and contradictions of a country which defies generalizations. There is, however, abundant evidence to show that we have arrived at a highly critical period, in which the whole may be sacrificed to a part, in which, through lack of considering the question in all its bearings, the mistakes from which the education of men in India has not been wholly free may be repeated and intensified in the case of the women, and in which the opportunity of developing a national system in line with modern educational science may be lost.

The present volume is an attempt to sift this evidence in the different localities visited, and to give, in so far as is possible to a writer who has no expert knowledge of Indian problems, an accurate description of the conditions of girls' education, and of the three contributing factors, the Government, the missionary, and spontaneous Indian effort. Where other localities have been treated the intention has been to show that the same factors and, to a certain extent, the same problems prevail. The survey is in no sense exhaustive; the State of Bhopal, which doubtless presents many interesting features, is not included. The great districts of South India and the Madras Presidency, where women's education is well developed, have unfortunately had to be omitted, and any generalization made must be taken with this reserve. The geographical division has been adopted, not because the same problems do not to a certain extent repeat themselves but because of the varying environment in which they are cast through diverse religious and social influences. A brief historical survey is included to indicate the general situation as well as certain outstanding features which are present throughout the whole country. No constructive theory is offered, but the need of such in relation to the moving life of the East and the impact of Christianity upon it is made apparent.

The moral and religious problem lies at the basis of all education and is at the present moment that most acutely felt in India. A system perfected in every technical detail and embracing the whole country would prove a disintegrating and disastrous force if it lacked the religious basis for the training of character. Yet its provision through the highest revelation of religion is fraught with immense difficulty in a country of diverse and conflicting faiths. A secular policy for the education of boys has already produced its fruits, and may serve as a warning in the new feminine problem. In a final chapter this question is touched upon in its relation to the ultimate Christianization of Indian thought and life.

II

HISTORICAL SURVEY

"We have now before us in that vast congeries of people we call India, a long slow march in uneven stages through all the centuries from the fifth to the twentieth."

THE history of the education of women in India must keep in view the three conflicting ideals of womanhood which have dominated Indian society at different epochs. These are the Vedic, the Moslem, and the Christian or Western. While our main concern is with the last, a brief glance into the early ages is necessary for a full comprehension of the conflicting currents found in the modern epoch. In the early Vedic times women apparently enjoyed an equal status with men. There was no child marriage, no seclusion in the zenana, no *sati*, no prohibition of the remarriage of widows. Ladies of culture composed hymns and performed sacrifices as men did. Some even remained unmarried and had their share of the paternal property. There are many passages in the Brāhmanas which show the high esteem in which women were held. Gārgā Vāchaknavi, a learned lady, is mentioned as taking active part in a great assembly of learned men summoned by Janaka, King of the Videhas, to decide which of them would prove the wisest. There is a celebrated conversation between Yajnavalkya and his learned wife Maitreyi on the possible comprehension of the infinite by the finite.[1] "One poem, the Bhagwan Manu, prescribes a positive punishment for parents who keep away from school their boys after five and their girls after ten years of their respective ages."[2] It would appear, in fact, that girls had some share in whatever education was available.

From about the fifth century B.C. in successive Hindu codes we find limiting laws, many of which were embodied about A.D. 200 in the Code of Manu. Their stringency is only weakened by a general recommendation that men "who seek their own welfare should always honour women on holidays and festivals with gifts of ornaments, clothes, and dainty food." The possibility of education was closed by the exclusion of girls from the initiatory caste rites, which served as a prelude to the education of boys.

"The nuptial ceremony is stated to be the Vedic sacrament for women and to be equal to the initiation, serving the husband equivalent to the residence in the house of the teacher, and

[1] *Cf. Ancient India.* R. C. Dutt.

[2] *Vedic Quarterly*, 1911.

the household duties the same as the daily worship of the sacred fire." [3]

"For women no sacramental rite is performed with sacred texts, thus the law is settled; women who are destitute of strength and destitute of the knowledge of Vedic texts are as impure as falsehood itself, that is a fixed rule." [4]

Fixed rules and settled laws do not always remain so where women are concerned, and there is considerable evidence that the women of the upper classes could often read and write, and, though the perusal of the sacred literature was denied, they certainly read and memorized the great popular epics, the Rāmāyana and the Mahābhārata, which embody many Indian traditions and ideals. In the Ajanta caves, which cover a period from the second to the seventh century A.D., women are represented as engaged in study with books of palm leaves. Elsewhere they are referred to as musicians and artists. In the dramas of Kālidāsa about the fifth century the inevitable jest at the expense of learned women is current coin. The comic character says he must always laugh when he hears a woman read Sanskrit or a man sing a song.[5] Amongst the Rajputs, where status was determined by courage not literacy, the women held a high position. In the early days of the

[3] Manu, ii. 67. S.B.E. The Vedic Sacrament had for its object the study of Vedic texts.

[4] Manu, ix. 18. S.B.E.

[5] *India through the Ages*. F. A. Steele.

nineteenth century the records of these early periods were carefully searched by Indian enthusiasts to produce evidence of former literary achievements as an argument for the introduction of Western education. A lecture by Pyari Chand Mittra, a Government schoolmaster, offers an interesting list headed by the famous Lilavati, after whom a mathematical treatise of the ninth century is named. Either she was the authoress thereof,[6] or it was specially composed for her perusal. "Besides Lilavati there were many females of literary and scientific attainments. The Tamils boast of having possessed four female philosophers: viz. Avyar and her three sisters. Avyar was the daughter of one Bhaguvan, a Brahman, and outshone all her brothers and sisters in learning. 'She was contemporary with Kumbur, the author of the Tamil Rāmāyana, and she employed her eloquent pen on various subjects, such as astronomy, medicine, and geography; her works of the latter description are much admired. Avyar remained a virgin all her life, and died much admired for her talents in poetry, arts, and sciences.' I am given to understand by an intelligent Hindu gentleman, that he knew of one Hātta Vidyalancar, a female scholar at Benares, who was versed in Smriti[7] and Nyaya. We also hear of the literary proficiency of the wives of Kālidāsa and Kornut, Raja of Khona, the latter was conversant with astronomy and is well known by the sayings she has left

[6] *India through the Ages.* F. A. Steele.

[7] Smriti = tradition (of philosophy).

behind; of Gargu, the wife of Yagnya Valkya, who is said to have possessed a good knowledge of Yog [8] Shastra." [9]

With the Moslem conquests came the *parda* system with its withering influence. Devised by Mohammed, according to modern Moslem historians, for the protection of women in wild and lawless times, it has inculcated distrust of their character and capacities. In spite of the fact that many Indian women to-day look upon the *parda* as a sign of prestige and of their value in their husbands' eyes, the thoughtful observer must reckon it, in its ultimate social influence, as a symbol of distrust. "A man both night and day must keep his wife so much in subjection that she by no means be mistress of her own actions; if the wife have her own free will, notwithstanding she be sprung of a superior caste, she will yet behave amiss" runs a later Hindu code, coupling this statement with minute regulations as to doors and windows. Isolated Indian women, both Hindu, and Moslem are prominent in later times, but they by no means represent the common life. Their chronicle is written because in some way or other they have been exceptional. In the thirteenth century it is said of Razia Begum, the only woman ruler in her own right of Moslem India, that the severest scrutiny of her actions could reveal no fault save that she was a woman.[10]

[8] System of philosophy.

[9] *Calcutta Review*, September 1855.

[10] *India through the Ages.* F. A. Steele.

The Calcutta School Society ascertained in 1818 that no provision of any kind existed for the education of women, and an attempted estimate of their general literacy places the figure at one in a hundred thousand. The old ideal had so utterly vanished, that it needed the touch of Western civilization to revive even the conception of its former existence. This existence, shadowy and faint though it may appear in our eyes, is an enormous asset to the new movement in a country where everything Aryan and Vedic counts for much in the endeavour to create a national consciousness.

The modern epoch is thus in part a Renaissance, in part the introduction once more of the ideal of another faith. It will occupy our attention in detail and falls naturally into three periods. The first dates from 1819, when the Baptist Mission in Calcutta started its first school for girls,[11] till 1854, during which time the influence was almost entirely that of the women missionaries; the second, from the famous Educational Despatch of 1854 till 1884, is characterized by the Government policy of "grants-in-aid" to voluntary associations, by the first tentative beginnings of direct Government effort, and by the expansion of Secondary education under missionary auspices; in the modern period dating from the presentation of the report of Sir William Hunter's Commission in 1884, the Government share in girls' education is much

[11] *History of Missions in India.* J. Richter.

more direct, the spontaneous Indian element enters more strongly, and for the first time the question of a differentiation in the curriculum arises.

The first period is essentially the day of small things. The Danish missionaries of the eighteenth century had included girls in their schools but there is little record of their doings, and the schools organized by Miss Cook in Calcutta (1821) and Mrs Wilson in Bombay (1829) were in every sense pioneer work. Elsewhere is to be found the full story of opposition, of fluctuating desire, of tactful consideration and of careful enlistment of enlightened Hindu men, who had been touched by Dr Duff's educational work, as advocates of the cause. The same discrepancy between theory and practice which marks the advocacy of some of the Indian social reformers of to-day existed then, and the movement was by no means an extensive one. By 1840, Miss Cook (now Mrs Wilson) records about 500 girls at school in Bengal of whom half were in her own school. Dr Duff in outlining a missionary and educational policy for India, points to the need of a great development of the education of men before that of women could possibly follow. "The education" of the latter "on any great national scale must, from the very nature of their position, which those only who have been in India can at all adequately comprehend, follow in the wake of the enlightened education" of the former.[12] Events have justified

[12] *Biography of Alexander Duff.* George Smith.

this prediction and in many senses it is true that the present state of women's education in India corresponds to that of the men in 1854. The education given by the women missionaries consisted of such mere rudiments as were possible under the conditions and for the short period during which their pupils were available. Simple instruction in the Scriptures was also given. Madras and other centres followed slowly on the same lines. The work was in part linked with the ordinary mission work of the Churches and in part carried on through separate women's societies founded for the purpose in Germany and in Scotland. At first the Government attitude was distinctly negative, except for the cordial personal assistance given by Lady Hastings to Miss Cook, and the more nominal support of her successor Lady Amherst. In 1849, however, Lord Dalhousie informed the Bengal Council of Education that henceforth its functions were to include female education, and the Bethune School which had been privately founded by a legal member of Council, the Hon. Drinkwater Bethune, was brought under the control of the Government. In the Bombay Presidency things developed more rapidly and the Parsi influence asserted itself in independent effort. The first municipal schools for girls were probably started in 1850 at Ahmedabad. In 1852 a second stage of missionary education was reached by the establishment in Calcutta of a Normal School for the training of Christian female teachers under the auspices of the society known later as the Zenana Bible and Medical Mission. The special method adapted to Indian conditions was not discovered till 1854, when the system of zenana-visiting, combined with educational instruction, was inaugurated in Calcutta by the Scottish Mission with the help of a clever Eurasian lady, Miss Toogood.

By the great educational charter of 1854, the Government adopted the policy of fostering and encouraging private effort by a system of grants-in-aid to all institutions which could comply with certain stipulations as to buildings, number of teachers, text-books and type of instruction given. Religious instruction might be given but did not come within the purview of the Government officials. Departments of Public Instruction were formed, Inspectors appointed, and the well known scheme of examinations inaugurated. It is stated in the Despatch that female education shall be given "frank and cordial support." "The importance of female education in India cannot be over-rated, and we have observed with pleasure the evidence which is now afforded of an increased desire on the part of many of the natives of India to give a good education to their daughters. By these means a far greater proportional impulse is imparted to the educational and moral tone of the people than by the education of men." In the main the Government adhered to this principle, yet considered it prudent to withhold its hand from direct interference with so delicate a matter. Whereas, in order to improve the school system as a whole, Government erected boys' schools in many places, to serve as models in management and efficiency, very few girls' schools were founded. The Circular order of 1868, issued under Lord Lawrence, states that "unless female schools are really and materially supported by voluntary aid, they had better not be established at all." In pursuance of this policy the Bengal Administration Report for 1881 notes only two Government Primary schools for girls, 719 aided, and 107 unaided voluntary schools. The women's missionary agencies in Calcutta were drawing a monthly grant of two thousand rupees for educational work. An Inspectress[13] was at this time in the service of the local education authority for the inspection of *parda* schools. Her note that "every day brings signs that the demand for female education in Bengal is slowly advancing and extending" marks the rising tide. Two exceptions may be noted to this policy; the exceptional activity in the district of the North Western Provinces (as they were then called) round Agra, and the movement of the Central Government under the influence of Miss Carpenter.

The Agra experiment was, however, the response of Government to spontaneous Indian effort, and as the work of the Hindu pioneer who

[13] Appointed to the Subordinate Educational Service in 1876. India Office Note.

was its originator is little known, the following account may be quoted.[14]

"Even in our Asiatic Provinces, before the breaking out of the troubles, a desire had sprung up among the natives to extend the blessings of education to women. Gopal Singh, a Hindu gentleman, holding under Government the post of district Inspector of native schools, had succeeded, through his own exertions, in establishing upwards of two hundred seminaries for young ladies in the Province of Agra which were attended by 3800 girls of the best families. By many of our countrymen in India, this is regarded rather as a social revolution than as an educational movement. As a rule, the natives look with suspicion on everything which comes from a foreigner, for which reason the great efforts made by the English have not produced corresponding results. 'The establishment of a little school,' observes the Pandit, 'which my own daughters and those of my immediate friends and relations attended at first like a charm, dispelled in a great measure the prejudices of my neighbours, and induced many to send their girls also. This example and my constant persuasion and reasoning have at last succeeded in inducing many respectable inhabitants of other villages to yield.' And so the movement bids fair to become national. The pupils are nearly all Hindus belonging to the more respectable classes. The teachers are all men."

[14] Popular Education in the North Western Provinces. —*Government Report*, 1860.

" 'Want of female teachers,' says Gopal Singh, was one great obstacle in the way; but the guardians of the girls composing the respective schools pointed out men of an approved character, in whom they have full confidence, and I have appointed such persons only as teachers; the result is very satisfactory.' "[15] The Government official note on the experiment is that the lack of the humanizing influence of trained school mistresses, and the impossibility of supervising the elderly Pandits were the real causes of the failure of the schools and not the Mutiny, which hindered the general development of education in the province but little. Accordingly the attempt was renewed in 1858 by one of the masters of the Agra College, a Jat[16] of good family, in co-operation with Government. He succeeded in securing "school mistresses of high caste and relatives of rich and influential zemindars,"[17] and by 1863, when he was appointed special Inspector of female schools, their number had increased to 144. The curriculum seems to have been somewhat different from that of the boys' schools, and the Pandit notes with satisfaction: "Girls are possessed of better memories and less selfishness than boys." The success and extent of the movement seems however to have been due to the personal influence of this one man, and with the passing of his generation the schools

[15] Popular Education in the North Western Provinces. —*Government Report*, 1860.

[16] An agricultural caste.

[17] Landowners.

degenerated in type. The rapid extension of this work under Government into other districts necessitated the employment once more of men teachers. Four female Normal schools were established which appear to have been such only in name. Two British Inspectresses were appointed whose reports indicate the same problems as those of a more modern date. "The villagers are not opposed to the schools but they value them chiefly as a means of support for Brahmans and relatives."[18] They could not believe that the Government were in earnest on the subject, when the girls' school was accommodated in a place not more attractive than a cow-shed and the boys' in a handsome building. In 1876, a drastic reduction of 212 schools took place and the question of female education dropped into abeyance for a period. The official comment thereon was that the State had incurred much expense in founding and maintaining these schools and that the results had been painfully disappointing. Historically, the experiment indicates the danger of extending girls' schools beyond the desire of the community and beyond the possibility of constant supervision on the part of British Inspectresses. The solution of the ever present problem of a supply of teachers was only a temporary one, and the failure of the Normal schools was attributed largely to the lack of a British superintendent.

The influence exerted for the education of

[18] *North Western Provinces Report on Education,* 1875.

women in India by Mary Carpenter, is a curious episode in a life whose main work in England was to lead the way to a national system of moral rescue and preventive discipline for juvenile criminals. During the last decade of her life (1867-1877), she visited India four times, and by her personal influence and enthusiasm she greatly affected the Government attitude and turned the rising conviction of the Indian Theistic movements into the right channels. Her position at home secured her a direct hearing in Government circles and the rapidity with which she adapted her pre-conceived notion of taking some Indian girls home for training to the wiser one of female Normal schools in India, proved once more her extraordinary power of vision in social problems. Herself of an intensely religious temperament, the revolt from the crudity of much of the orthodox religious teaching of the time led her sympathies largely in the direction of Unitarianism, and believing, like Mountstewart Elphinstone and many other Christian Indian statesmen of the period, that secular education for India was ultimately the more religious policy, she threw her whole influcnce into the establishment of schools which would not in any way interfere with the religious beliefs of the people. Yet her attitude to the mission schools was warmly sympathetic and she notes her indebtedness to the accumulated experience there.[19] Some further

[19] *Life and Work of Mary Carpenter.* J. E. Carpenter, 1879.

provision, however, seemed necessary in the case of girls, as the boys of the country had larger opportunities and the social system was in danger of one-sided development.[20] Her whole energy went towards the foundation of female Normal schools and in 1867 she secured a grant from the Central Government of £1500 per annum for five years for the establishment of these schools in Bombay and Ahmedabad on condition that an equal amount was provided by the native community. This stipulation was in accord with the previous policy that Government action should not in so delicate a matter be in advance of native opinion. Mr Dadabhai Nauraji, in a letter to the Secretary of State for India, following on a memorial from Indians in London, gives a general survey of the income derived from the native endowments for female education in different parts of India at this time.

Bombay . . .	Rupees	40,000
Punjab . . .	,,	4,321
Madras . . .	,,	234
Bengal . . .	,,	132
North Western Provinces	,,	..

It will thus be seen that a certain response existed even if only amongst a few advanced sections of the population. Further direct contributions were not immediately forthcoming, but after various memorials a Government grant of £1200 for five years to each of the capitals of the three

[20] *Six Months in India.* Vol. I., p. 278. M. Carpenter.

Presidencies was ultimately given without this special stipulation. Miss Carpenter's scheme for the Normal schools laid special emphasis on the need of experienced English supervision and instruction as the only means whereby the proper training could be secured and the dignity of the teaching profession for women raised. The failure of the so-called Normal schools in the North Western Provinces and the success of the mission training schools in Calcutta proves the wisdom of this policy. The new schools passed through various vicissitudes, but ultimately, Miss Carpenter had the pleasure of seeing substantial fruit of her labours at Ahmedabad, Poona and Madras. Much of the interest she had aroused amongst the Indian community was doubtless sporadic, and many of the schools started were short-lived, but in the main her influence on the development of women's education in India has counted as a dominant factor in the Government policy, in the establishment of the National Indian Association and in the permanence of certain institutions.

The activity of Christian missions during this period seems extraordinary, when the difficulties which hampered Government efforts are considered. Moreover, all their educational work was handicapped, so far as numbers were concerned, by the frank and open avowal of the desire to win their pupils ultimately for Christianity. The missionaries had, however, at their command the one essential asset—Western women who were willing to give themselves heart and soul to the work. Eight new women's societies, both British and American, entered India between 1860 and 1870, and educational work both in zenanas and in schools was their most effective means of contact with the people. Their pupils in the Primary stages were drawn both from the non-Christian population and from the orphans and converts in connection with the missions. As it was possible to retain the Christian girls, and even some of the others for longer than the usual period, owing to the exclusion of men teachers from the mission schools, a Secondary system on identical lines with that for boys began to be slowly built up.

The Inspectress in the North Western Provinces notes that almost the only really prosperous Middle girls' schools are those in large stations superintended by ladies of the missionary societies.[21] Miss Carpenter's testimony to the schools in Madras and Calcutta is in similar terms. Where village schools were attempted they seem to have suffered from lack of constant supervision. In 1870, the Isabella Thoburn School, Lucknow, was founded, and in 1880, the Sarah Tucker School, in Palamcottah. In 1881, the Free Church Mission School in Calcutta had the satisfaction of passing a successful candidate for the First Arts examination. This girl, and a pupil from the Bethune School who passed in the same year, were the first in all India[22] to accomplish this feat.

[21] *North Western Provinces Report on Education*, 1877.
[22] *Ibid.*

The third period, from 1884 to the present date, is marked by a definite change in the attitude of Government. The Educational Commission of 1882 under Sir William Hunter revealed many abuses which had grown up in connection with the system in vogue for boys, and also showed how little had really been done for girls. The recommendation is that girls' schools should now receive "special encouragement and liberality." The further recommendation of the Educational Commission of 1900 is that girls' schools should receive liberal grants and that the fees should be less rigidly enforced. The standards of instruction in the Primary schools should be different and have special reference to the requirements of home life and to the occupations open to women. This policy, emphatically reiterated in the Despatch of 1904, has worked out differently in the different provinces, as is indicated elsewhere. Its main features in the last two decades may be said to be the appointment from home of experienced educators as Inspectresses of Schools in the Indian Educational Service, the establishment of model schools for girls like those formerly created for boys, in districts where the aided schools had not reached the required standard or did not satisfy the wants of the neighbourhood, and a considerably increased financial outlay both in grants and direct educational work. In 1907 the total expenditure amounted to over forty-four lakhs. There is no desire in any way to supersede the aided schools, on the contrary, it is recognized that the more their work is extended, so long as it is really efficient, the better for a country which like many others groans under its taxation, and where also the limit of desire for female education is still easily reached. To efficiency and adequate supply, the Government directs its attention. The proportion of the schools directly managed by the Public Authority to private or aided schools may be seen in the accompanying table, being slightly over 20.41 per cent. of the whole.

Of the aided schools there is no separate official classification to show what proportion are managed by Indian committees, and what by missionary agencies.[23] Where possible this has been indicated from local information in the chapters on the separate provinces. The Indian spontaneous element has become however much stronger during this modern period, not only in Bombay, where it has grown steadily since 1847, but also in connection with the various Samajes in the Punjāb, United Provinces and Bengal. The orthodox Hindu element is seen in the system of the Mahakali Pathshalas[24] started in Bengal in 1893, while probably the most remarkable feature in the Indian movement is the establishment of girls'

[23] The Madras Report alone gives separate figures:

Secondary schools,	Government,	2	Mission,	35	Indian,	0
Primary schools,	,,	208	,,	523	,,	331

[24] Pathshala = school.

MANAGEMENT OF GIRLS' SCHOOLS [25]

	Under Public Management.			Under Private Management.		Total.
	Government.	Municipal Board.	Native States.	Aided.	Unaided.	
Training Schools . .	12	2	1	44	4	63
High	7	—	—	98	7	112
Middle English . . .	3	1	2	179	6	191
Middle Vernacular . .	56	10	185	11	—	262
Primaries . . .	365	1,274	250	7,041	1,053	9,983
Total	443	1,287	438	7,373	1,070	10,611

[25] *Quinquennial Survey of Progress of Education in India*, 1907. Vol. II. Tables 181-184. These statistics include Eurasian Schools.

GIRLS UNDER INSTRUCTION CLASSIFIED ACCORDING TO RACE OR CREED [26]

	European.	Native Christians.	Hindus.	Mohammedans.	Parsis.	Buddhists.	Others.	Total.
SECONDARY SCHOOLS (High and Middle English)	11,502	10,725	4,316	140	1,402	757	552	29,394
MIDDLE SCHOOLS (Vernacular)	11	6,896	17,561	1,104	5	6,246	20	31,843
PRIMARY SCHOOLS (For Boys and Girls)	564	22,776	133,341	27,832	820	31,379	2,431	219,143
(For Girls only)	1,547	16,063	214,092	46,876	3,626	10,382	1,519	294,105
TRAINING SCHOOLS	173	844	292	70	—	32	9	1,420

[26] *Quinquennial Survey*, 1907. Vol. II. Table 180.

schools under committees of Indian gentlemen representing different faiths. This indigenous movement is due in part to a desire to provide a good education without direct interference with the religion of the pupils, and in part to a reaction from the extreme secularism and the Westernizing influences of the Government schools.

Missionary work in education during the modern period is marked by continued expansion. The former success of mission agencies in taking a proportion of their pupils beyond the elementary stages is redoubled. Of the forty three High Schools for Indian girls, only five in 1907 were under Government management. "The bulk of female Secondary education is provided by missionaries."[27] A glance at the religious classification table will show that out of some 17,000 Indian girls in the High and Middle Schools more than 10,000 are Indian Christians, while a large proportion of non-Christian pupils are also studying in mission schools and colleges. The Christian Primary schools in the villages have also greatly improved in type through the introduction in some places of modern eductional methods under the careful and regular supervision of trained English managers.

As we survey the situation as a whole, certain problems stand out as common to all India and as indicating how critical is the present period in relation to the ultimate development of her women. These are the extension of Primary

[27] *Quinquennial Survey*, 1907. Vol. I., p. 257.

education, the retaining of pupils in the higher stages, the nationalizing of the curriculum, the supply of teachers, and finally the place of the religious element in education.

In spite of the recent rapid increase and the steady progress of the last twenty years, the percentage of girls of school age attending school is only 4.6,[28] and though the next Quinquennial Returns will probably show a marked increase, the desire for education has still in many places to be created. The proportion of girls in the Secondary stages is not shown by the number of those studying in High and Middle English schools,[29] as many of these are in the Primary classes. Only 1208 girls were actually in the High School departments in 1907. In that year 178 girls passed the Matriculation examination.[30]

[28] Comparative Percentages. In 1886—1.6 per cent; in 1896—2.1 per cent.; in 1901—2.2 per cent.; in 1907—3.6 per cent.; in 1910—4.6 per cent.

[29] Schools are classified as

(*a*) Primary, including Standards I to IV.
(*b*) Vernacular Middle, including Standards I to VII.
(*c*) Anglo-Vernacular Middle or Middle English, including Standards I to VII. English taught from Standard IV.
(*d*) High, including Standards I to X. English taught from Standard IV and used as a medium in the higher stages.

This classification varies somewhat in the different provinces, especially as to the age for using English as a medium. (*b*) is entirely absent from some returns. (*c*) and (*d*) are often grouped together as secondary schools.

[30] *Quinquennial Survey*. Vol. I., p. 255.

This small proportion indicates, apart from the social and religious customs which cause it, a lack of balance in the whole system. Are the circumstances under which higher education is given not such as commend themselves to the Indian mind? Or is the course of studies pursued not of sufficiently practical and educational value to prove attractive to Indian women? Is there any foundation for the popular belief that the physique of Indian girls is not strong enough for a prolonged school course? These questions underlie much of the discussion in the following chapters.

Two causes are apparently at work. In India as a whole 42% of the girl pupils are studying in boys' schools. These naturally never proceed beyond the Primary stage, as co-education is not, except in the hill districts, in accordance with Indian ideas. There seems therefore a great need for increasing the number of Primary schools for girls only, whence the transition to the higher stages would be easy. In some districts there is practically an unlimited field for expansion in this way. Another cause may possibly be the difficulty of access to really first-class schools for non-Christian girls. The missionary societies which have done so much for the higher education of boys have, with certain exceptions, concentrated their attention on the provision of excellent boarding schools for the girls of the Christian community rather than aiming at developing a parallel system for girls

Government Examination of Girls, Calcutta

which would attract the non-Christian element, as it has on the men's side. The new Middle and High schools which are springing up under Government and Indian auspices are an attempt to meet this need, but there is undoubtedly room for further development.

The problem of the curriculum is a very subtle one. In the early days of the reform of girls' education in Great Britain, about 1862,[31] the greatest need seemed to be the adoption of an adequate test of knowledge, and that test one already recognized, so that there might seem to be no lower requirement to suit the supposed lower capacity of the feminine mind. The same principle worked in the early days of girls' education in India and preparation for Matriculation[32] seemed the only means by which the standard could be raised. Whereas in Great Britain the leading girls' High schools have developed a flexibility and variety of curriculum wherein many a "womanly woman" has found her training, even if she did not prefer to seek her education in one of the numerous excellent private schools, the girls' curriculum for Indian girls has been stereotyped on masculine lines. If we assume that education should prepare for future life, it seems clearly wrong that the preparation for spheres so totally different as those of Indian men and women should be identical. A highly trained missionary educator sums up the problem of the

[31] *Renaissance of Girls' Education*, A. Zimmern.

[32] *Cf.* Appendix A. for curriculum.

Secondary school as follows :—" In spite of the fact that less than 1 % go on to college, the whole plan of school education is made to lead up to Matriculation and instead of completing a school course, the aim is to prepare for a college course that is never entered upon." The Inspectress in Bombay writes in this connection :—" Such a course is harmful, and girls leave these schools with weakened physique and very little in the way of real culture to compensate for it." An Inspectress from Madras also writes :—" The examination shadow is to be seen in every room from the third form upwards, and it is only with the greatest difficulty that sufficient time can be snatched for the teaching of a little recitation, drawing and drill, in view of the annual inspection." In the Presidencies of Madras and Bombay a departmental examination is offered as alternative to Matriculation for girls, and in this such subjects as botany, hygiene, drawing, dress-making, cooking, appear as substitutes for algebra and geometry, but the schools prefer to send up their girls for Matriculation." The further question arises not only of the differentiation of the girls' curriculum from that of the boys' but also from that of Western girls. How is Indian female education to be brought into close touch with Indian environment ? The spontaneous Indian movement is in part an attempt to meet this problem, while on the other hand it inclines to view as a racial affront any suggestion to adapt the curriculum to the special needs of girls. The

Government Inspectresses are closely considering the matter and are eager to welcome any constructive policy which will lessen the danger of creating the "female Babu." Several missionaries are working hard against the denationalizing tendencies which in many cases were introduced before the reformed educational methods prevailed in the West. A conference of English educators and Indian missionaries was recently held in London to discuss Indian curricula and the relation of the educational problems of the East and West. It is true that the opinion of Indian missionaries is not yet unanimous on the need of any alteration, and as the bulk of Secondary education is in their hands their co-operation is essential. There is however good hope of a sound constructive theory being ultimately produced if women of sufficient courage, originality and ability can be found to plough for a while a lonely furrow. The curricula for the Primary schools is a different question. Some educators hold it to be the saner policy to accept the fact that the majority of the girls will only be at school for four years, and to adapt the whole course to this limitation. A correspondent of the Education Commission of the World Missionary Conference 1910, writes :— "Under such circumstances, therefore, the aim should be directed towards a sound elementary education in reading, writing and arithmetic, a knowledge of domestic economy and hygiene, and the formation of a strong moral character. The aim, that is, must be determined by the opportunities offered for education. It is better to reach a lower aim than to try for a higher aim and fail altogether. I believe the mistake that is made in regard to the education of Hindu girls is in attempting to do the impossible. There are many subjects which it is extremely desirable to teach, but the limited time during which the girls are teachable makes it imperative to concentrate on what is attainable. We should aim, therefore, at demonstrating to the people that the girls who have been to school become superior housewives and mothers; that what they learn is of real value to them in the home; and above all, that their moral character is improved and strengthened."[33] The Primary curriculum has already been remodelled to a certain extent. In Bengal, Eastern Bengal, and the United Provinces separate schemes have been issued. In the two former the courses follow the method of the Kindergarten in the lower classes, and include much nature study, also hygiene, domestic economy and sewing. In the United Provinces and Bombay the reading-books in use for girls are different. These reading-books are often the only printed matter which a village girl may ever possess, and they are intended to impart a large amount of useful information. A reformed curriculum in the hands of untrained teachers becomes, however, a dead letter, perhaps hardly less injurious than the mere literacy of former

[33] *World Missionary Conference Report.* Vol. III. p. 51.

days, and thus the interdependence of the various educational problems is once again illustrated. Is it advisable to increase the number of Primary schools, and to adapt their curriculum without an adequate supply of trained teachers ?

The problem of the teacher can be traced since the first beginnings in 1820, recurring with the same baffling insistency. The modern situation shows little advance, except that the absolute necessity of having all teachers to some extent trained is gradually being recognized, and grants are influenced by the degree in which this ideal is kept in view. The sources of supply for teachers in Indian schools of all grades are women from English-speaking countries, Anglo-Indians or " country born " English girls from the Hill schools, members of the Brāhma and Ārya Samāj, Indian Christians, Parsis, married women of some education from the Hindu non-Brahman community and lastly " women who have learnt to read and write at home." This last class is still astonishingly prevalent. Teachers from other sources are sometimes procured but, except in the case of married women, they are few in number. There are also a good many elderly pandits teaching in village schools. The trouble is that the demand enormously exceeds the supply. Here is a dilemma familiar to missions. A village school has no teacher ; there is at hand a mission pupil, who has finished her Vernacular Middle Examination, but has not been trained ; too often it ends in the appointment of the girl to the school, as the committee knows that the interval before she marries will be only too brief. This illustration applies throughout the mission field. The difficulties, moreover, attending proper chaperonage of village mistresses are enormous. The employment of widows, where such are forthcoming, is subject to the same difficulty, but ultimately they may with proper training and care become a main source of supply. The hopes which early theorists have built upon the widows of India are to a certain extent already justified and may still be confidently cherished. As regards the opportunities for training, a special circular, issued by the Central Government, in 1901, has provided a needed stimulus to both official and private effort. It is difficult to distinguish absolutely between Secondary and Primary training,[34] as some institutions have a few students doing more advanced work than the others. On the whole there is a distinct lack of provision for the separate Secondary training of women teachers; very few women graduates have taken it and the creation of the opportunity might create the demand. The students in training are mostly Anglo-Indian. The provision for Primary training is more adequate, though there is still in some instances a lack of that co-operation between missionary societies which would lead to more efficient work. The details of management and religious classification of pupils are given on pages 48 and 49. The

[34] *Cf.* Appendix B.

great difficulty in all the Primary training work is the lack of preliminary knowledge; in some of the institutes for widows, indeed, this is a long forgotten minimum. The influence of the previous curriculum upon those who pass on to the proper Vernacular Course after the Middle Examination is also felt. An experienced teacher comments :—"The shadow of prescribed examination which hangs over the school course before training tends to leave the girls quite unacquainted with the newer subjects, and they are not able to acquire these during their training course with sufficient thoroughness to teach them satisfactorily afterwards."

The inter-relation of these problems needs to be borne in mind throughout. It seems in many ways as if the whole reform in women's education in India must begin from above downwards, namely in the High School and College stages combined with Secondary training, till the impulse imparted thence is felt throughout every grade. This subject is specially treated in the chapter on the University Education of women. Reform further can only come through closer co-operation, the need and opportunity for this will be apparent in the course of our study of conditions in the different provinces.

III

BURMA

" Thou son of *dewas* ; to hear and see much in order to acquire knowledge ; to study all science that leads not to sin ; to make use of proper language ; to study the Law in order to acquire a knowledge of propriety of behaviour ; these are blessed things, *Dewa*, mark them well.

" Thou son of *dewas* ; to be patient and endure suffering ; to rejoice in edifying discourse ; to visit the holy men when occasion serves ; to converse on religious subjects ; these are blessed things, *Dewa*, mark them well."

The *Mingala-thut*. Buddhist Beatitudes.
(Burma—Sir George Scott).

IN Burma the ancient ideal of Indian womanhood may still be seen in a somewhat purified form. The Buddhist faith which gives a touch of gentleness to every relation of life, has accentuated its best features and swept away many of the laws which hindered its development elsewhere. There is thus very little in the position of women in Burma at which even the most pronounced feminist could cavil. The woman is, if anything, the predominant partner and yet few realize that she rules. Gay, blythe and débonnaire, the sunniest spot in a sunny scene, her rainbow-tinted tamein relieved by a short white jacket, a coloured scarf across her shoulder, and fresh flowers clustering in her dark lustrous hair, the Burmese woman is ready any day for any problem of life you may choose to propound. She is the bargainer, trader and financier of the family, and as such her legal and monetary position after marriage is well assured. Marriage is here an affair of the heart, and it is entered upon when young life flows strong in the later teens. A woman may not marry without her parents' consent before the age of twenty, but then if marriage is her wish, why should the parents not consent? Why should anyone object to anything which promises to fulfil the heart's desire of another So runs a contented "laissez faire" policy. And life is not measured in terms of money by the Burmese. If education has a chance anywhere of being regarded not as a means of livelihood but as a leading forth of the mind to higher and nobler thoughts, it is here in Burma, in consequence of the mental characteristics of the people. Work beyond what is needed for the bare necessaries of life seems unnatural, and there is no perpetually rising standard of comfort, nor passion for accumulation to bind the Burmese to an unceasing wheel of toil. He pauses to be glad and to rejoice. The art of rejoicing is one of the chief arts of Burma, and there is perhaps no country in the world where it is carried to such a pitch of perfection. No generalization can be made about any people unless long years are spent in their midst, but the first impressions made by the Burmese on a stranger generally confirm the writers who characterize them as modern hedonists. There are books which show another side of the picture, and many sad facts (notably the looseness of the marriage tie [1]) bear them out, but leaving these aside, and turning to our particular problem, we find that the girls' schools of Burma are glad and happy places. There is an atmosphere of buoyancy and quiet zest in work which strikes the visitor at once, and this testimony is amply borne out by the teachers.

It must, however, be remembered that not all girls in school in Burma are Burmese. A large proportion of them are drawn from the Karens, who occupy the tracts of hill country on the frontier of Lower Burma, in Tenasserim, and in the Delta of the Irawadi. The gradual civilization and raising of these tribes to the standard of the Burmese in general, is on all sides attributed to the excellent work of the missionaries, (the American Baptists and the Anglicans). Where Christianity comes its special social results follow. There is a Chinese community numbering over 40,000 and a strong Mohammedan section, not to speak of Hindu immigrants from South India, Tamils and Telugus, while the variety of the educational problem may be seen in the

[1] "Marriage in Burma is simply concubinage, which may terminate at the desire of either party." *Christian Missions in Burma.* W. C. B. Purser.

Girls at St Luke's Mission, Toungoo, Burma

official enumeration of the other races under instruction: "Karens, Talaings, Chins, Shans, Danus and Inthas, Chinese, Indians, Palaungs and Taungthus." The interior of Burma is inhabited by about fifty-seven different tribes speaking forty different languages. Feminine education however is not as yet a matter of importance amongst the hill tribes; apart from the Anglo-Indian (Eurasian) schools, which lie beyond the province of this book, it affects mainly the Burmese, Karen, Chinese and Mohammedan communities.

As regards general literacy, Burma ranks high in the provinces of the Empire; the proportion of girls at school to girls of school-going age was 9.6% in 1910,[2] as compared with 4% in 1907 in British India as a whole. This distinction is however mainly in the Primary stages, for the women graduates of Burma can so far be numbered on one's fingers. It is also entirely confined to those areas which have come into touch with modern civilization. There are large tracts of hill country where the women are totally uneducated, for the Burmese and Karen women alone contribute to the high proportion. One would however naturally expect to find a well developed system of female education throughout the various stages, offering possibly an example to the other provinces, and it is surprising to find that this is not the case. On the contrary there is considerably less organization and no such

[2] *Public Instruction Report, Burma*, 1910.

definite policy in female education as in Eastern Bengal. The real reasons for the creditable proportion are the later age of marriage, the bright temperament and ability of the Burmese girl, the complete absence of *parda*, and the general social atmosphere, which permits girls to study unhindered in boys' schools throughout all the stages. Thus there are more girls studying in boys' schools than in separate ones, viz. 73% as compared with 42% over India as a whole. The system seems in many ways to work well. Of the three contributing factors, which are found in every province, the work of Government, the spontaneous Indian movement, and missionary effort, the last overwhelmingly predominates in Burma, especially in the higher stages.

The policy of the Government, more especially as regards girls' schools, has been to encourage, guide, and, to a certain extent, finance private institutions while undertaking little direct work of its own. As will be seen from the accompanying table, only four institutions are directly under the Central Authority. A certain proportion of girls may also be found in the Government and Municipal Secondary schools for boys; the Primary schools for boys directly under public control only number fifteen and the proportion of girls in them is therefore a negligible quantity. No Inspectress or Assistant Inspectress has as yet been appointed, partly because funds are lacking and also because, apart from purely domestic subjects there does not,

MANAGEMENT OF GIRLS' SCHOOLS IN BURMA [3]

	Under Public Management.		Under Private Management.			
	Government.	Municipal Boards.	Aided by Government.	Unaided.	Number of Scholars on Roll.	Number of Girls in Boys' Schools.
College	..	..	..	..	..	12
High	..	..	9	..	1,523	502
Middle—English	..	..	16	..	1,968	1,086
Middle—Vernacular . . .	4	..	48	..	3,312	9,456
Primary	..	..	619	..	20,022	40,534
	4	..	692	..	26,825	51,590

Note.—Deducting the Anglo-Indian figures it leaves only 676 Indian girls taking High School Education.

There are also 86 Private Institutions of an elementary character with over four thousand pupils.

[3] *Public Instruction Report, Burma*, 1910.

seem such a crying need for it as in other parts of India.

The spontaneous Indian element may practically be identified with the Buddhist educational movement, except for one small Mohammedan school in Rangoon where tiny girls learn the Koran. To Buddhism and the Buddhist monks may be attributed the high standard of literacy in Burma as a whole. Practically every Burmese boy knows how to read and write, and he has learnt it at the monastery.[4] In the nature of things girls are not admitted to these *Kyaungs*, but there are apparently some parallel schools for girls, conducted by nuns. "Besides the monastic public schools, there are private schools kept by laymen and occasionally also by women, in which girls as well as boys are taught."[5] The private institutions which do not come under inspection are mainly of this character. One fruit of the recent Buddhist revival is the Empress Victoria Buddhist Girls' School, which owes its existence and tone to the energies of Mrs Hla Oung. Her main idea is the combination of modern education with definite instruction in Buddhism and in this the school differs from all the other indigenous girls' schools, where little beyond bare literacy can be acquired. Excellent education up to "Anglo-Vernacular Standard VII" can be obtained here under competent mistresses or masters. An Anglo-Vernacular school has also

[4] *Missions in Burma*, p. 13. W. C. Purser.
[5] *Burma*. M. and B. Ferrars.

recently been opened through private generosity for the girls of the Chinese Colony in Rangoon. There is naturally no spontaneous and independent effort for girls' education among the hill tribes, though in many cases they are ready to meet the missionary more than half-way.

The missionary influence in the education of girls in Burma is thus a most important one, and includes every stage from the Kindergarten to Normal training. The chief agencies at work are the American Baptist Mission, the Society for the Propagation of the Gospel, and the Methodist Episcopal Church of America. The Roman Catholic educational schemes exist largely for the Anglo-Indians and the Tamil immigrants from South India.

The American Baptist Mission dates from the time of Judson (1810), and has now in connection with it over 70,000 native Christians speaking eight different languages. The educational scheme for their Christian girls is very thorough, and leads up through a system of small village schools to their Burmese boarding school in Kemmandine, a suburb of Rangoon, and to an excellent mixed Karen school, also in Rangoon. There is a separate Normal school, and one or two especially clever girls are to be found in the Matriculation class of the Baptist Boys' High School preparing to go to the Mission College. A large proportion of the non-Christian girls are drawn into these schools by the efficiency of the education offered. The centre of the S.P.G.

work is St Mary's School, Rangoon, which dates back to 1865, and is a first-class institution in every way. It is satisfactory to note that several of the staff are former pupils who have returned to teach here, after training in the S.P.G. Normal School. Some of the staff are Anglo-Indian, but a good proportion are Burmese Christians. Two English ladies are in charge. There are about one hundred boarders, mostly Christian, but including some Buddhists, and nearly an equal number of non-Christian day scholars. The school works under the Government Code, and earns an excellent grant. There are three other good S.P.G. schools for Burmese or Karen girls which lead up to St Mary's. Those at Toungoo and Mandalay have a considerable number of boarders. A few of these are drawn from the immigrant population—as Kansi, the little Ghurka girl in the accompanying illustration. Her father is a Christian, and contributes regularly to her maintenance. The policy of the S.P.G. Mission seems, so far, rather to concentrate on a few good schools than to develop much village educational work. The Methodist Episcopal schools, like those of the S.P.G., are partly for the Anglo-Indian community, and partly for the indigenous population. In Rangoon they have two good High schools, one of each type, and other schools in the country. The educational work done by other societies in Burma is not extensive; but, where every unit counts, it has its own contribution to make. There are arge tracts of hill country round Burma

Ghurka Girl Boarder at S.P.G. Girls' School, Mandalay

which are still waiting for missionary advance, and where the women are totally uneducated. The pioneer work to be done would be of the type usual amongst primitive peoples, and might produce the same magnificent results as amongst the Karens.

Passing from the organizing agencies to the actual pupils, the religious classification as seen in the accompanying table is of interest.

The Anglo-Indian pupils pass through the various stages of their education in the High School, hence their absence in the statistics of the Primary schools. The proportion of Mohammedan girls in the High schools is striking, and is possibly due to the fact of mixed parentage; Buddhist freedom to a certain extent influences Mohammedan customs in Burma. By the new regulations only 15% of the places in the "European" schools are available for Burmese or Indian girls, and these vacancies are eagerly sought after. The curriculum pursued in the various schools is laid down in the Government Code, and there are no schools of any importance which stand apart and develop an experimental curriculum of their own, as occasionally happens in other provinces. Burma has, as yet, no University of her own, and the curriculum of the schools with the corresponding departmental examinations is to a certain extent determined in relation to the Calcutta Matriculation. Schools are classified as "High" in which after a good vernacular foundation, the pupils are taken up to Matricula-

CLASSIFICATION BY RACE OR CREED OF BURMESE SCHOOL GIRLS[6]

	Europeans.	Native Christians.	Hindus.	Mohammedans.	Buddhists.	Parsis.	Others.
High School	1,349	14	9	23	31	25	72
Middle—							
Anglo-Vernacular	470	453	6	28	1,001	2	8
Vernacular	4	543	38	114	2,938	..	1
Primary	128	1,121	77	208	18,481	..	7
	1,951	2,131	130	373	22,451	27	88

[6] *Report of Public Instruction in Burma*, 1910, p. 41.

tion, English being used as a medium of instruction in the higher forms; "Middle Anglo-Vernacular," in which English is taught orally from the Primary stages and as a written language from the fourth class, instruction is given only up to the test of the seventh standard, and in the latter stages English is used as a medium; "Middle Vernacular," in which pupils are taken up to the seventh standard, but no English instruction whatever is given; and "Primary," where vernacular education is only carried to the fourth standard.

The curriculum is in many respects very similar to that found in schools at home, and is open to the usual criticism that its influence is denationalizing. A recent order limits the teaching of English in the first three classes to simple conversation lessons, in order that more stress may be laid on correct vernacular. The advantages of the oral method in the hands of a skilled teacher are undoubted, but it is a question whether the Department have not been somewhat premature in this respect. The Kindergarten classes are excellently conducted in some schools, and every effort is made to keep them as Burmese as possible in character. In drawing, a complete series of copies based on Burmese design and ranging from the most simple to the most elaborate, has been prepared and is in extensive use. It is when the stage of optional and alternative subjects is reached that the denationalizing element enters more strongly. In one High school visited, only about 25% of the girls were taking Burmese, in some forms only one pupil did so, while many of them take Latin, and a preponderating proportion choose English history as being an easy examination subject. The number of Anglo-Indian girls partly explains this choice. Indian history is a compulsory subject throughout, and the Government Code offers ample scope for vernacular and classical Oriental study. It is the choice of the individual pupil or parents which is at fault. Sewing is not a subject which carries a Government grant, and excepting at a few of the European schools, it is at a low ebb. The Principal of the S.P.G. High school acted as Inspectress for the Department in this subject during 1910 in some twenty-six schools, and through her efforts the standard has been to some extent raised, but there is a crying need for a properly appointed Inspectress, who will develop this subject as well as a sound system of instruction in hygiene and domestic economy adapted to Burmese conditions. The tendency is for the girls to drop off in the higher forms at about sixteen years of age, so that very few really go up for the Matriculation examination, and these mainly with intent to teach. Others pass after Standard VII. straight to the Normal school.

In outer circles a strong destructive criticism is directed against the anglicizing tendency of education in Burma, but amongst the missionaries actually engaged in it there is not the same realization of a possible need for change as is found amongst certain sections of missionary educators in other parts of India. The reason for this may partly lie in the fact that the Western education of girls—indeed education at all beyond the mere rudiments—is of later date in Burma than elsewhere, and that consequently its full effect cannot yet be traced. Moreover, among the Burmese there is not the same "nationalist" spirit as exists in India proper, and this directly influences the educational problem. It must be remembered, too, that there is not the same gulf between the woman's life and the man's as in other parts of India, and that the system used for boys may in many respects be excellent for girls. But whether we have here in its early stages a problem which is destined to become more acute, is a subtle question and one worthy of close inquiry. At any rate, no constructive theory has as yet been put forward by any mission school. The general public, however, criticize, and taking that criticism for what it is worth, there is a general indictment on the ground of the education given being mere "cram," and not really a training of mind and character. A Burmese Deputy Commissioner writes: "If women have become more educated, many have also become more frivolous, spending their time in reading songs, *zats*,[7]

[7] Dramatic tales with pointed moral. The "Pyazats," the modern development thereof are popular burlesque plays, performed at festivals. *Cf. Burma.* Sir George Scott.

and useless trash, instead of doing more useful work."[8] A special accusation is also directed against the general atmosphere of the school, which is too reminiscent of English to be the natural one for a foreign country.

Both these criticisms are apparently concerned more with the problem of the teacher than with that of the curriculum. The Government Code is elastic, the trouble is the lack of emphasis laid on Oriental subjects. A British or American missionary may often enter at once into school life in Burma without any opportunity of knowing the people or the language, and be thus unable to give the Burmese tone, which in theory she may or may not value. I observed the special case of a young American at the head of a large Anglo-Vernacular Middle school who was obliged to interview her new pupils through an interpreter, and had no means of supervising the instruction given in the vernacular throughout her school. The educational problem translates itself here into the mission problem of understaffing. It may doubtless be argued that the denationalizing influence in the mission schools is that of a religion presented in its Western aspects but it is interesting to note that the same atmosphere is felt in the Empress Victoria Buddhist Girls' School,[9] which is constantly under the personal influence of Mrs Hla Oung, a leading Buddhist. The definite statement, "We wish to be English in everything except our religion,"

[8] *Public Instruction Report*, p. 18. [9] *Cf.* p. 66.

affords a striking contrast to the care with which some missionaries seek to preserve all that is good and right in national tradition and custom.

Passing from the dominant influence to the staff, through which the Head-mistress must transmit her ideals, what opportunities of training have these teachers had ? As regards the Normal schools the whole work is practically in the hands of the missionaries. There are four Normal schools for girls all under mission management. These included in 1910 eighty-eight pupils, of whom sixty-nine were native Christians. There are also a few girls in the Government Normal schools for men, notably two Mohammedan girls in the Mandalay school. The criticism in the Government Report is that the literary work demanded of the female students is too severe, especially if they do not aim at teaching in any institution higher than a Primary school. Some alteration in the curriculum is suggested. Moreover, many teachers cannot afford to defer the opportunity of an immediate salary, and do not pass through the Normal school. Most of those in charge of the mission schools, however, insist upon Normal training for their teachers. The type of teacher produced is not, according to general opinion, a very high one ; she is intellectually weary, and looks upon her career mainly from a pecuniary point of view. There are, of course, marked exceptions. Teachers' Associations do not exist, and it is questionable whether these would be advisable owing to the heat and strain of the necessary hours of teaching. The material, therefore, with which the Headmistress has to shape her school is not of the best quality, and it is all the more necessary that she should have leisure from routine for personal contact with both pupils and staff. This is just what she does not get. A very large proportion of her time is often taken up by work on Government schedules, and in personally teaching the higher English classes. In mission schools, which frequently have non-Christian teachers on their staff, she may also have to teach the Scripture lessons throughout. So far, we look in vain for Burmese women who have passed up to the University to train as leaders. Of the twelve women Arts students in Rangoon, only one is Burmese. She is a Christian. Even the Anglo-Indian community, from which many of the teachers are drawn, rests content with the qualification of First Arts (a two years' University course), and no graduates have, as yet, to the writer's knowledge, taken Secondary training. The ideal for women's education in Burma is the production of some fully qualified Burmese Head-mistresses, who will be able to impress their individuality on the whole system, and thus make it contribute to the beauty of their national characteristics.

It will thus be seen that the day of foreign and missionary educators in Burma has in one sense only begun; they are needed for pioneer work amongst the untouched hill districts; for the even more difficult task of guiding the course of higher education into the right channels; and for the work of training those who will prove in the future its best interpreters to their own people.

IV

EASTERN BENGAL AND ASSAM

"A woman's place in the National life will now best be filled by the realization of herself; she must grow to her full stature, taking as her due her share of God's light and air, of the gifts of the Earth-Mother."

C. SORABJI.

TO pass from the sunny smiling country of the Burmese to Dacca, the capital of Eastern Bengal and Assam,[1] is to enter a scene of strange contrast, and one marked by monotone and inertia. The brilliant Eastern sun shines down, but its rays are caught by no golden roofs and domes; sombre grey stone meets the eye, with here and there traces of the carving and colouring left by the alerter men of centuries ago; there are no smiling happy groups of women busy with the day's work, their gay garments bright against the background of tropical green, but only here and there ghostly figures clad in *burqas*,[2] or some scantily draped "sweeper"

[1] This was written before the Durbar Proclamation on the further re-adjustment of Bengal areas. Calcutta is now the capital of the Bengali-speaking districts.

[2] White veil with eye-holes, enveloping the whole person.

women, little heeding, and as little heeded. A strange town it is, with a strange mixture of civilizations, and yet possessing withal a certain charm of latent capability. Relics of a Hindu past are there, almost lost beneath the Moslem dominance of the thirteenth century, which brought with it some of the glory of architecture and the learning of Upper India, but seemed to take on the colourlessness of the land to which it came, winning chiefly the lower classes ; now the new Western influence has come, and has given to the Bengali, by means of education, a unity which repudiates its source, thus creating a young India awake and alert. The diverse characteristics of the capital are in a sense typical of the diversity of the whole province and of the problems of its administration and development. The new province created by the Partition in 1905 includes the territories formerly administered by the Chief Commissioner of Assam, to which have been added certain districts lying on the Eastern side of the bay of Bengal, the river regions of the Padua and the Jumna, and the Chittagong division which borders on the Burmese hill district. It thus includes large city populations, such as Dacca with over 90,000 inhabitants, and great river districts such as Sylhet, and the PaduaMeghna Delta, with its intersecting channels, which in the rainy season multiply by the hundred till the country is a network of waterways, and in which every brown boy is as much at home as he is on land—a country of villages and of rich abundant harvests, where the monsoon fails not, and famine is unknown. Then there are the hill districts—the Khasi and Garo Hills, the native states of Manipur and Tippera, and the country bordering on Burma, where a strong and vigorous people, marked by a hardy independence, are only gradually being touched by modern civilization. While the educational problem is mainly a rural one—in 1901 only 2% were enumerated in the sixty one towns—the urban minority, with its demand for higher education, cannot be ignored.

Female education in Eastern Bengal has certain aspects which make it differ from that in other provinces, and render it a peculiarly interesting study. Whereas elsewhere we shall trace the development of the three different influences—the spontaneous Indian movement, missionary efforts, and the work of Government, the last, in varying degrees, a unifying and co-ordinating agency—here we have one well-organized Government Female Education Committee, on which all these interests are represented, and by which a unified policy is in process of being worked out. This Committee was appointed after the Partition in 1907, to work under the Director of Public Instruction, and consists of those officials directly concerned, of non-officials of various creeds, of representatives of several missionary agencies, and of a few Indian and British ladies selected mainly for their interest in such matters. It is in no sense a popular body, and it has no executive function;

A Hill School, Eastern Bengal

but it has done some extremely useful work. Its policy has been to survey the field, taking into account the diverse and complicated nature of the task to be accomplished, to utilize so far as possible all existing agencies, and to plan a thorough and scientific scheme embracing all classes. The development of this scheme must be one of slow and patient labour. No great social scheme which is to have permanent results can be enforced in a revolutionary or sudden way, and least of all where prejudice has to be overcome, where public opinion must be influenced, and where possibly the passing of generations and the influence of heredity are needed for its fruition. In a sense the very backwardness of the province is its opportunity. The possibility before it of laying foundations on sound educational principles, of using the experience gained by other provinces in the adaptation of certain types of institutions to local conditions, of surveying the whole field without haste, and of making a systematic effort to raise all classes and all sections of the population, augurs well for the future standing of the province, and may produce a better type of education than that which has developed more quickly and more sporadically elsewhere.

A sketch of the present situation must naturally take as its centre the work of this Committee, the result of its survey of the classes affected, its utilization of existing agencies, its constructive work, and the practicable character of its aims.

What, then, of the actual girls to be educated?

The classes affected are many and diverse, education and rank often varying in inverse proportion; the educational and the social problems are here again so closely interwoven that the holding of parda parties has a very definite relation to the statistics of school attendance. The Indian Christians, of whom there are over 66,000, mostly living in the Khasi and Jaintia Hills are naturally keenly eager for education, and contribute considerably to the supply of teachers. About the non-Christians it is impossible to generalize.[3] From the young Begum [4] directly descended from one of the Moslem invaders to the child of some peasant woman, who grudges her from the work of the field to the seemingly profitless village school, is a far cry, and the gamut of possibilities lies between. Here is a high-born Moslem girl, whose male relatives hold University degrees and Government appointments, and who will allow a certain advance to their women-folk, but no more. For instance, an English teacher may be admitted for a few hours a day, or if the family be wealthy and of sufficient rank, an English governess may be secured to devote her whole time to the pupils. Here is another still so tied by conservatism that she may not see English ladies or learn of modern thought. Her male relatives may give her the

[3] Mohammedans, 18 millions. Hindus, 11½ millions. Animists, 1¼ millions. 1901 Census.

[4] This title is used of a Mahommedan woman of a ruling family, or who can prove direct descent from the Prophet.

smattering of Koranic lore which is necessary for religion. The Mohammedan women of the upper class can nearly all read Urdu, and are clever with their needles. Here is a girl of the Brāhma Samāj, supposed to be free, and yet one might almost say shy of her freedom, with every opportunity to take the higher education which would fit her for social influence, she yet ceases her studies when only some three standards beyond her Hindu sister. Another girl with the same up-bringing has sufficient strength and determination to persevere through the whole course and finish with Normal training or University honours. There is a strong demand for education up to a certain stage also among the Brahmans, Kayasths,[5] and Baidyas,[6] a demand which is, however, limited to the few years before the *parda* is strictly drawn, an event which happens between the ages of eight and eleven. Then there are the lower class Mohammedans, who are anxious only for Koranic education, the Namasudras,[7] whose intellect is at so low a level that a whole term may be spent in acquiring a single letter of the alphabet, and the hill tribes where *parda* is non existent, and where in certain cases the women are more literate than the men. The whole enumeration shows how very diverse

[5] A literary caste.

[6] A literary caste, about 25 per cent. of their women are literate.

[7] Descendants probably of the original inhabitants of the district.

and complex are the classes for whom education must be planned.

Passing to the agencies at work, there have been in the more advanced portions of the province, apart from Government and the municipalities, spontaneous efforts to educate girls. Some of the present village schools are of this indigenous type, and are kept possibly by an elderly Hindu pandit and his wife, where little girls are collected for a few hours daily—not stated hours—and drone over Bengali books of an archaic type, in an ill-ventilated room. The result of this education may be the ability to recite certain shlokas [8] and to check a marketing account, or merely the prestige in the marriage market of having been to school. Where it is possible to improve schools of this type or standard, they fall into the general scheme, but as a rule they are "passed by on the other side." The Mahakali Patshala,[9] started in 1907 at Mymensingh, represents again spontaneous effort of a more advanced type, and is an attempt to give a modern and strictly religious education on Hindu lines. This institution is much more advanced than the parent Patshala, described on page 113. The Mohammedan community have been more backward in organizing schools; a circular sent out by a Sub-Committee on behalf of the Government to

[8] Shloka, a particular type of Sanskrit metre, often used loosely to mean any verse of Sanskrit poetry.

[9] Patshala = school.

various Mohammedan associations produced very few replies, including the following: "But it is not proper time for starting Mohammedan female education, as the people are not willing to have their girls educated." There is, however, a certain number of Muktabs or Koranic schools, where girls are taught what is necessary for religion, and in some cases a little secular knowledge.

The most important missionary agencies in the province are the Baptists from Australia, New Zealand, America, and England, and the Welsh Presbyterians, all of whom are carrying on good educational work. The Sisters of the Oxford Mission have also entered the field more recently. Taken as a whole the missionary contribution is, however, much smaller than in other provinces. The best vernacular school for girls in Dacca is that which has a hostel attached of the English Baptist Mission, and the training of teachers at Nowgong in the hill districts is proving specially useful to Government. This can be better considered later in relation to the hill districts as a whole. The mission schools are a welcome addition to the educational scheme, and it is satisfactory to note the cordial relations and co-operation between their organizers and the Government officials. As regards their extension, if new schools were contemplated in a town or district where a good accessible school already existed, grants would probably not be given, but as the field is practically unlimited, the question is merely academic.

Thus the constructive policy of the Government Committee[10] embraces these existing agencies and all schools entirely under public control, whether municipal or directly under Government. The Committee aims at the ideal of a Primary school in every village, in more populous centres the raising of a certain number of these to schools of a rather better type, the establishment of a Government school (Middle or Anglo-Vernacular) in the headquarters of every division, the warm encouragement of all private Middle schools, and the development of some definite system of *parda* instruction which could reach the higher and stricter classes. The system is completed by three existent High schools. Taking these different stages in order we must first consider the Primary schools.

There were in 1909, 4501 Primary schools in the whole Province, an increase of about 800 on the preceding year. Assam and the Surma Valley are scantily provided. The establishment of a sound system of Primary schools is naturally the chief aim, but its attainment depends on the development of a thoroughly efficient staff of teachers. The word "primary" covers a multitude of sins, and is very varied in its application. Here, for instance, is a school of the aided type in a village of over 6000 inhabitants. The little girls are crushed together on ill-constructed benches in an ill-ventilated room, agonizing in

[10] Information throughout is chiefly drawn from *Proceedings of Female Education Committee.*

different degrees of shyness under the thrilling ordeal of a visitor. All of them are Hindus, for the Mohammedans do not go to school in this village. Apparently there is scarcely any system of classification except for the broad distinction of "little" and "less." All are under eleven years of age and, according to the village custom, have walked to school in charge of the school servant. The school is supposed to teach up to Standard III, but every girl who leaves able to read and write, and not much injured in health from sitting daily for five hours in a cramped position, may consider herself lucky. The attempts of itinerant Sub-Inspectors at teaching the venerable pandit how to teach, have fallen on unscathed shoulders, yet there is a certain pathos in the owl-like glance with which he fixes the two Sub-Inspectors, who answer all the visitor's questions without the least reference to him. For the pandit knows that his day is done—a new school is in process of erection, and an energetic Sub-Divisional Officer is on the outlook for a trained schoolmistress. With the passing of the pandit will go much of the quaintness of the Indian school, which sentimentally may be regretted, but which must yield place to the modern demand for efficiency. It is refreshing to turn to a school of the new order, an urban one. The day is wet, so only twenty-five out of forty pupils are present, Hindus chiefly, of the Kayasth caste. The three lowest classes are happily seated on matting with a tiny desk in front; the older ones are still swinging their feet on too high a bench—but what good is there in having Inspectresses if there is nothing to improve? A tidy time-table on the wall shows the rotation of lessons. There are shells for arithmetic, maps and object-lesson sheets, there is space for drill or breathing exercises at the end of every hour, there are neat specimens of sewing (not perennial ones which have survived many an inspection) and above all, there is a happy smiling mistress, whose personality inspires new ideals and new thoughts. A bright little maiden of eleven in a blue and gold sari, who gaily translates an Urdu conversation into Bengali, has designs on a scholarship for the Eden High School, and perhaps some day she, too, may be an "Ustani"[11] as wondrous wise as her mistress. This is the bright side of things, but it shows the possibilities which lie under dry statistics. The recent report of 1910 on Primary schools in the town of Dacca shows an increase of about 200 girls in one year. Of the sixteen schools, twelve are now provided with mistresses and the general progress is satisfactory, although there are still many difficulties to overcome, especially if the proportional increase in the number of pupils exceeds, as is probable, that of the trained teachers available, and proper space is lacking. The problem in Dacca is typical of the urban problem throughout. Primary education in the hill districts is of a different type.

[11] Teacher.

The Middle Schools, partly English and partly only vernacular, are some twenty in number, varying in type from a long established school such as the Alexandra Girls' School at Mymensingh, with ten teachers, and a Headmistress from the Isabella Thoburn College,[12] to one which has only six scholars beyond the Primary stage and one mistress, but which must be raised in standard and type for the sake of the district. The generosity of the native landowners is to be noted in connection with these schools; in two cases a whole new building and site have been acquired in this way.

All roads lead to Mecca, and all pursuit of higher education in Eastern Bengal tends to the Eden Girls' High School, Dacca, where, under the supervision of Miss Lena Sorabji, the portals of Calcutta University are successfully reached. This school is the Model High School for the province, the two others at Chittagong and Mymensingh are not as yet so efficiently staffed or equipped, though that at Chittagong holds its own at the Matriculation examination. There are some two hundred girls in the Eden High School, mostly Hindu, with a fair proportion of Brāhma Samāj and Mohammedan girls, including also a few Christians. The curriculum is that of a first-class English High school in its relation to the Matriculation subjects. In the lower classes the scientific principles of education are in full vogue, story and group method, with an excellent

[12] *Cf.* p. 137.

Kindergarten apparatus. The teachers are mostly Indian with three Anglo-Indians, and there is also a very efficient music mistress. Moral instruction is given, and there is throughout an excellent tone. It is possible to attend the school and keep strict *parda*, a young Begum has recently been assigned to it by the Court of Wards in order to complete her education. A very important feature of the school is the Training department, in which teachers are trained for the Bengali-speaking parts of the province. (Assamese teachers are trained at Nowgong and the Hill Districts in Shillong.) Training is given free on condition of teaching in a Government school for two years thereafter. There is both an English and a Vernacular course, and the effect of the latter can be seen in such schools as the Primary school sketched above. There are three students at present in the English department, and twenty-two in the Vernacular. Any girls passing the Matriculation examination from here are certain of Government scholarships, or "stipends" as they are called, to the University of Calcutta. The only drawback at present is the lack of space, but plans are already definitely formed, and a site secured for new buildings, which will ultimately include a College department.

But when all is said, it is only an infinitesimal fraction of the female community which is touched by the Middle and High schools. The fourth sphere of the Committee's work, the organizing

A High School Class, Eastern Bengal

of a definite system of *parda* instruction, is therefore in some ways the most important. Many important and far-reaching influences are at work behind the veil, and it is here, too, that the influence of the Education Committee must be felt. A comparison of the numbers attending Primary schools (84,798) with those attending High and Middle schools (1846), shows how limited is the school period for the average girl. The *parda* instruction to a certain extent supplements the education of those children who are withdrawn for marriage at about ten years of age. On the other hand, as the number of girls of school age at school is only 3%, a certain amount of this work is amongst the absolutely illiterate older women, though the minimum age of ten prevents overlapping with the Primary schools. A further aim is to create a more friendly atmosphere in the zenanas towards the whole question of education. In some cases it is an immediately fruitful work, in others a sowing of seed for the future. There are now some 600 girls and women under instruction of this type in seven different towns, the classes in Dacca being most fully developed. Here there are four governesses at work, each with six centres to teach. Two of them are Mohammedans, one Brāhma Samāj, and one Christian, the last under missionary superintendence. The education given is of the simplest type, including, however, in some cases drawing, painting, history, and geography. Indeed when the circumstances are taken into consideration it could hardly be otherwise; the classes are held in the houses of progressive men, rich or poor, and consist as a rule solely of the women of the household and their immediate neighbours, the numbers varying from six to about twenty. The ages of the pupils vary from eight to fifty, all are at different stages, all are irregular in attendance, many are accompanied by babies, and the class generally ends in individual instruction. Yet progress is being made, and it is good to see the group of daintily dressed women awaiting the arrival of the teacher who forms their link with the outer world. A very great deal depends on her personality and skill in overcoming prejudice. One of the teachers is a Mohammedan lady of good position, the wife of a pleader; she drives in strict *parda* to and from her work, and has naturally inspired other strict Mohammedans with confidence in the scheme. Recently an English governess has begun work in Dacca under the Committee, but in her case there is a binding fee of five rupees for every family who employs her. The system is one which is peculiarly adapted to Eastern Bengal with its strict *parda* customs, and though expensive to Government,[13] is in the meantime more than worth while in its indirect influence in breaking down prejudice and supplementing the whole system of instruction.

[13] 50 rupees per month in addition to 25 rupees gari-allowance is given to each governess and the pupils do not contribute much.

Education in the Hill Districts reveals a somewhat different problem. There is no *parda*, co-education is frequent, and suits the customs of the people. A Lushai writer dealing with this says: "The men and women are all on the same footing, except in some cases, where the women are master." In the hill tracts of Assam, some 2551 girls are studying in boys' schools and 701 in separate girls' schools, practically all of the latter and a large proportion of the former are worked by the missions, which are doing excellent service to education. The schools are much appreciated, and the Government grant of 4022 rupees to the mission schools is almost equalled by the contributions of the people themselves. Special arrangements are being made by Government with the American Baptist Mission at Nowgong for the training of Government teachers in the Mission Training School. In some parts education is absolutely at a standstill; for example, in the Mikir hills, "female education is supposed to have perished fifteen years ago with the death of its only representative, a young girl of Nowgong!" In Chittagong Hill District the opposition is that of a wild uncivilized people. A boarding school is the only possiblity, but that seems too terrible! The parents are half-civilized, and will send a child for one month and withdraw her the next; the children, moreover, have their own way. "If the parents say their girl shall go to school, and she says 'I will not,' she does not go." There are at present seven precious pupils in the Mission Girls' school at Chandra Ghona. In Tippera there is much opposition. Twenty-five girls are, however, reported in three mission schools in the latter district. An interesting account of indigenous schools comes from a lady missionary working in one of the hill districts: "There are some small Primary independent village schools taught by Hindu men or women voluntarily. Some of these receive Government aid, and some do not. The parents of the scholars contribute a little towards the teacher's support, and supply the school-house. It is generally believed that the visits of a missionary to such schools lend prestige to them, and the children are encouraged to attend by the small rewards given by the missionary for attendance and Scripture knowledge. Hence such scholars invariably welcome regular visits." The main problems are those of co-education, the training of teachers, and the multiplicity of dialects. Steps are also being taken to develop weaving and local industries in many parts for the less advanced tribes.

Such in brief outline is the Government policy for female education. How far is it a living reality? "The moment imagination has gone out of your Asiatic policy, your Empire will divide and decay."[14] How far is there imagination in the educational policy? How far is it magnetic, flexible, and inspiring? A policy, of necessity, is reflected by the persons who

[14] *Indian Speeches.* Lord Curzon.

administer it, the inspectorate and teaching staffs, the organizing Committee, and the general social attitude of the community. The task of the Inspectorate is no easy one, and the word calls up visions of many successive nights spent in bullock carts, in trains, and on horseback to reach the inaccessible parts of an inaccessible province, a multitude of detail, and little time to relate it consciously to the underlying principles. To the casual onlooker taking into account the general social conditions of Indian life, it hardly seems work which a woman should do, and yet it is work which must be done by women. Indian girls can only be well taught by women, and this necessitates a female Inspectorate at least for the upper grades. From 1908 to 1911 there was only one Inspectress in the province, and in 1909 two assistant Inspectresses were appointed; an additional appointment has, however, recently been made for the Chittagong and Surma Valley Districts. A further increase would greatly facilitate the development of the work, and would probably repay in efficiency the extra expense. There is a great deal written and said about the denationalizing influence of education, and the need for bringing our system into touch with Indian thought and Indian life. More especially in the present case, when a new policy is being shaped, there is need for flexibility in the system and an Inspectorate closely in touch with the inner side of Indian home-life. What should an Indian girl know? What will fit her best to hold aright her true place; what will render her happier and more intelligent, retaining her Sita-like devotion and her gentle bearing? The planning of a curriculum and teacher's manual in relation to this aim is no easy task, and it remains to be seen whether the new manuals, the work of the first Inspectress, will have fulfilled these demands. Some women are born teachers, and some have teaching thrust upon them. In India the old ideal of teaching is that of a vocation; the bread of life is given freely by those who have to those who have not. Modern conditions have of necessity modified this ideal to a certain extent, but its spirit is still needed. The great scarcity of women teachers, and consequent certainty of employment, tends to lower the standard of character and efficiency. The teacher who will only do her own "kām,"[15] and not lend a helping hand to others, who is ever listening for the stroke of the clock, who is quick to take offence and ill to conciliate, is known in this province as elsewhere. The lack of a common religious basis as a ground of appeal is undoubtedly felt; the establishment of Teacher's Associations in the urban centres, and, where possible, of the Young Women's Christian Association Teachers Union, might be useful. It is to be regretted that very few of the teachers are not drawn from the families of upper class; the work done by one of the Mohammedan governesses in Dacca is an evidence of what can be accomplished in this way even without scientific

[15] Work. "It is not my work" is a common excuse.

training. There are, however, some splendid Indian women teachers, contact with whom is an inspiration, and it is to be hoped that the influence of the training classes in the Eden High School at Nowgong and at Shillong may gradually raise the general tone. Here, as in Burma, is the great means of counteracting anglicizing influences; education is the communication of personality, and the ideal Indian school of the future must have Indian teachers. The instilling of the principles of educational science and of true culture in Indian teachers, until these are no longer slavishly reproduced but lived and worked out in relation to Indian environment, is the task of the Western educator.

The success of any policy depends upon how closely it is in touch with the spirit of the community, and the wisdom of connecting a local committee with the management of every Middle and High school is unquestioned; these Committees are supposed to consist of equal numbers of men and women, and indeed the Government grant is often given only on condition of there being an efficient working Committee. There are also ladies' committees in connection with the zenana classes in the urban centres. It has, however, been exceedingly difficult to secure the necessary ladies for this work, for the supply of educated Indian ladies is very limited, and English women, because of the shortness of their stay in any one district, are unwilling to undertake it. Some of the officials' wives have, however, given splendid service in this way, and even if it is only a passing service it is more than worth while. The work of these committees in the breaking down of social prejudice and ensuring the confidence of the community is untold. There is, as has been already said, a definite connection between *parda* parties and school attendance. The *parda* party as a social institution in other provinces has come to stay. It is perhaps a pity that here it has had a certain shadow cast upon it of officialdom and organization. The spontaneous and individual effort is quickly felt and appreciated by Indian ladies. It must come also from a genuine and mutual desire for intercourse and not from any *sous-entendu* motive of pity or "bridge the gulf" idea. Indian ladies have their own contribution to make to the unifying of ideals not only between Indian and English, but between Indian and Indian. "The less said about *parda* parties and the more held," is probably a wise dictum. The work on some of the educational sub-committees will, however, often give an English lady the direct contact with Indian life which is so much needed.

The outlook for women's education throughout the province is in many respects a hopeful one; enthusiasts are working at it, there is a steadily increasing flow of girls coming to the schools; a teaching staff is gradually being built up, suitable text-books and manuals are being produced. The generosity of a Government, hampered by finance in every way, to this scheme, is a stamp of warm approval. No great social undertaking, however, is fulfilled in haste, and least of all where sympathy and the silent influence of individual friendship are needed to pave the way for it.

V

BENGAL

> " My Motherland, I sing
> Her splendid streams, her glorious trees,
> The zephyr from the far-off Vindyan heights,
> Her fields of waving corn,
> The rapturous radiance of her moonlit nights,
> The trees in flower that flame afar,
> The smiling days that sweetly vocal are,
> The happy, blessed Motherland."
>
> Translation by W. H. Lee, I.C.S.

ONE of the subtlest problems of sociology is to trace the relation of cause and effect in new conditions of life affecting a community. Here in Bengal is a certain group of people calling themselves " a new nation "; here is a new thought-centre by turns indefinite, immature, bombastic, tentative, yet possessing a certain unity and aspiring after certain definite ideals, and together with it, in part as cause, in part as effect, is the steady educational advance of certain sections of the community. There is little geographical unity, for the term " Bengal " has been of varying content, comprising in the early days all the East India Company's possessions in Northern India; after 1836 a more definite and limited area, and finally[1] in 1905 reduced, broadly speaking, to Bihar, Chota Nagpore, Orissa and the section of Bengal proper which lies west of the Ganges and the Hooghly. Ethnically, a mixture of Dravidian, Mongolian and Aryan elements, even linguistic unity, is lacking, Bengali, Hindi, Bihari and Oriya, with their corresponding dialects being the languages mainly in use. Yet, in spite of all, the Bengali claim of unity is there in virtue of their education, and in virtue of the "high proportion of literacy that exists in Bengal compared with most parts of India." Linguistically again, Bengali, though only the native tongue of some 52%[2] of the population, has become a modern literary language, and as such is a strong factor for unity and progress. It is true that those conscious of this unity who express themselves variously in congresses, in journalism, in sedition, or in loyal Government service are doubtless a minority, but they are an increasing element, and one which may assert itself more in the future. The political side of this movement is beyond the scope of this book, its existence cannot, however, be ignored as it is one of the causes of the tide which is slowly setting in favour of the education of women.

All the same obstacles and difficulties which we have studied in Eastern Bengal, and some even more hard to surmount, are to be found here. Seventy-eight per cent. of the popula-

[1] *Cf.* Note Chap. IV, p. 78.

[2] *Imperial Gazetteer of India*—Volume *Bengal.*

tion are Hindus and the consequent custom of marriage below the age of ten years cuts short the possible period of school attendance for girls. One woman in every five is a widow, and yet custom and prejudice prevent this numerous class from entering the teaching profession, as is the case with many spinsters at home. Ninety-four per cent. of the population live in scattered villages, and this increases the financial difficulty of providing sufficient accessible schools for girls whose parents are unwilling and often unable to pay anything. A strong prejudice against the whole idea of the education of girls still exists, and though systematic efforts are made to overcome this, they often lead to no result, as is testified in the report of a Mohammedan gentleman of good position engaged by Government to popularize education among his co-religionists in Bihar. It often seems as if all effort to overcome this prejudice were unavailing. Yet in the face of all this there is a strong body of Indian opinion which emphasizes in speech and in the press the need and advisability of female education. The Brāhma-Samāj, one of the reform Indian sects much tinged by Christian thought, gives every opportunity of education to its women, and has thus an influence out of all proportion to its numbers[3] in the province. By the extremely orthodox Hindu it is looked upon with the same suspicion as Christianity, and yet its tenets of liberty and equality

[3] Only 3171 in the 1901 Census.

for womanhood have a direct bearing on the general *parda* conditions, especially in the cities, so that, while the overwhelming proportion of girls over twelve years of age in school is Christian or Brāhma-Samāj, the influence of a new movement is beginning to make itself felt. An occasional Moslem girl, to whom a Government "stipend" has been awarded for her encouragement, is to be seen in the higher classes, or a young Hindu widow, who has been allowed to return to school to fit herself for a useful life.

Historically this movement in the Indian community is the result of the work of Christian missions, which have been consistently the leaders both in producing a high educational standard amongst the Christian women and in affording facilities to any others who would come to their schools. The Maharani of Baroda gives a fitting tribute in her recent book[4] to Miss Cook and Lady Amherst as the two pioneers of women's education in all India. Some share of this should also be given to Mrs Marshman, under whose instigation a society for the Education of Native Females was founded in Calcutta in 1819. In the same year the first modern girls' school in all India was opened under its auspices. By 1821 thirty-two pupils were in attendance. Though the Baptists were the first to actually start instruction, a parallel movement had been made by a united committee of British and

[4] *Position of Women in Indian Life.* Her Highness the Maharani of Baroda. *Cf.* also Chap. II, p. 36.

Hindu men. This Calcutta School Society was founded in 1818 to advance the education of both boys and girls, and on its invitation Miss Cook left England to open a school for Hindu girls in Calcutta. The courage of the Hindu members of the committee, however, failed them when it came to the actual starting of the school. "Although they had spoken well while yet the matter was at a distance and in the region of theory, they recoiled from the obloquy of so rude an assault on time-honoured custom. The Babus had been brought up to the talking-point, but not to the acting-point." [5] India thus lost the honour of a direct share in the first Western education of her women. Miss Cook was fortunately able to transfer her services to the Church Missionary Society, and opened her first school in 1822. The dramatic circumstances of this are worth quoting in full: [5]—

"Whilst engaged in studying the Bengali language, and scarcely daring to hope that an immediate opening for entering upon the work, to which she had devoted herself, would be found, Miss Cook paid a visit to one of the native schools for boys, in order to observe their pronunciation; and this circumstance, trifling as it may appear, led to the opening of her first school in Thunthuniya. Unaccustomed to see a European lady in that part of the native town, a crowd collected round the door of the school. Amongst them was an interesting looking girl, whom the school

[5] *Calcutta Review*, 1855.

pandit drove away. Miss Cook desired the child to be called, and by an interpreter asked her if she wished to learn to read. She was told in reply that this child had for three months past been daily begging to learn to read with the boys, and that if Miss Cook (who had made known her purpose of devoting herself to the instruction of native girls) would attend next day, twenty girls should be collected. Accompanied by a female friend conversant with the language, she repeated her visit on the morrow and found fifteen girls, several of whom had their mothers with them. Their natural inquisitiveness prompted them to inquire what could be Miss Cook's motive for coming amongst them. They were told that she had heard in England that the women of their country were kept in total ignorance, that they were not taught to read or write, that the men only were allowed to attain any degree of knowledge, and it was also generally understood that the chief obstacle to their improvement was that no females would undertake to teach them; she had therefore felt compassion for them, and had left her country, her parents, and friends to help them. The mothers with one voice cried out, smiting themselves with their right hands, 'Oh what a pearl of a woman is this!' It was added, 'she has given up every earthly expectation, to come here, and seeks not the riches of the world, but desires only to promote our best interests.' 'Our children are yours, we give them to you.' 'What will be the use of learning to our girls, and what good will it do to them ?' They were told :—'It will make them more useful in their families, and increase their knowledge, and it was hoped that it would also tend to give them respect and produce harmony in their families.'—'True,' said one of them, 'our husbands now look upon us as little better than brutes.' Another asked, 'What benefit will you derive from this work ?' She was told that the only return wished for was to promote their best interest and happiness. Then said the woman, 'I suppose this is a holy work, and well pleasing to God.' As they were not able to understand much, it was only said in return that God was always well pleased that His servants should do good to their fellow creatures. The women then spoke to each other in terms of the highest approbation of what had passed."

In the course of 1822 eight schools were established, attended more or less regularly by 214 girls. The Marchioness of Hastings also created a deep impression by personally visiting many of the back alleys of the city, and during the last two years of her stay in India her enthusiasm did much to allay prejudice. In 1824 the Ladies' Society for Female Native Education was formed through the efforts of Miss Cook (now Mrs Wilson), and a handsome central school was erected, to which Indian gentlemen, notably Raja Buddinath Roy, contributed largely. Lady Amherst was the first President of the new society. Dr Duff, commenting on the situation some twenty years later, marks the wisdom of the middle course between the "impossible" and the "all things possible" party, the courage of those who were willing to begin with "here and there a few." While he held that the education of the men of India must precede the education of the women, on any great scale, he looked forward to the time when "there would be a wide and spontaneous demand for female education by thousands and ten thousands. Then indeed would dawn upon India the golden age of education."[6]

It is a far cry from those days to the Calcutta of to-day with its seven High schools, five of which have college departments, its Training College, its Female Inspectorate, and a Government eager to do anything to promote what it regards as a main social factor in the development of the country. The "rising tide" may be best studied in comparative percentages.[7] As in Eastern Bengal, three forces are working here for the

[6] *Address on Female Education in India*, 1839, delivered by Dr Duff at the First Annual Meeting of the Scottish Ladies' Association.

[7] Percentage of girls of school age at school.

1881 . . .	0.87
1891 . . .	1.61
1901 . . .	1.8
1910 . . .	4.3

The total number of girls under instruction is now 171,569.

Imperial Gazetteer. Bengal Public Instruction Report, 1910.

Management of Schools for Indian Girls in Bengal, 1909-1910

	Under Public Management.			Under Private Management.	
	Government.	District or Municipal Board.	Native States.	Aided.	Unaided.
High Schools	1	..	..	7	3
Middle—English	..	..	..	12	1
Vernacular	..	..	..	17	2
Primary	86	1	25	2,508	429
Training	1	..	..	14	..
Total	88	1	25	2,558	435

Bengal Public Instruction Report—Statistics pages 4 and 32.

education of women, the Government, spontaneous Indian effort, and the missionary societies, and a brief analysis of these with their varying types and functions may serve to throw light on the general situation with its problems and possibilities.

The Government system is a somewhat different one from that employed in the newer province of Eastern Bengal and Assam, and may be taken as the normal one in the various provinces of India. The work is directly under the Director of Public Instruction, and forms a separate section of the ordinary Educational Department. There are two Inspectresses, who are members of the Indian Educational Service, but a large proportion of the inspection in the country districts is of necessity done by the ordinary Inspectors. Eastern Bengal has here the advantage of newer and more plastic organization. The Government policy is rather to aid voluntary schools than to launch out on schemes of its own; its influence is mostly felt as a unifying agency by means of Code, standard of examination and inspection, and as presenting occasionally model types to which the voluntary schools may or may not think it wise to conform. Thus less than one in twenty-eight of all girls' institutions are entirely under public management, as may be seen in the accompanying table. A slight divergence from this policy may, however, be noted in the increase of Primary schools directly under

Government control from one in 1907 to eighty-six in 1910.[8]

The Bethune Girls' College and High School, Calcutta, founded in 1849, may be taken as a type of a model Government institution.[9] Situated near Hadua Talau in the heart of the native city, like all city schools it suffers from lack of space. There is a fine pillared verandah through which one enters into an open court. Into this court open all the class-rooms. A characteristic feature is a very fine and spacious library well stocked with the classics of East and West. At the time of my visit several girls were sitting at work in it. A marked difference between Indian girls' High schools and those at home is that many of the former in the *parda* districts aim at having a College Department, which is affiliated to the University and in which girls are prepared up to the B.A. stage. The merits of this system will be discussed elsewhere.[10] In the Bethune College Department there are about thirty-five students, and in the school proper some one hundred and fifty, ranging in age from tiny girls of five or six to the Matriculation candidates of sixteen years and upwards. The lower classes are extremely crowded, and there is the falling off in the upper school which is so characteristic of India. This presents one of the most difficult problems in the education of Indian women. The aim being to fit the pupils for life, and to train them to think,

[8] *Imperial Gazetteer*. [9] *Cf.* Chap. II, p. 36.
[10] *Cf.* Chap. IX.

how can it possibly be accomplished in the three short years which in the majority of cases is all the time available? In the High school proper the assumption is that the girls will stay on, and the Bethune curriculum is shaped accordingly. There is a good Kindergarten, and all the modern plant to make an efficient school; the great drawback, as usual, is the lack of trained teachers, only one of the whole staff having full qualifications. Indian music is well taught as an extra subject, and it was a pretty sight to see some half-dozen girls accompanying the harmonium with violin, *escar*, and *zitta*. The school owes its success to two factors, first the personality of its former Head-mistress, Miss Bose, the first woman graduate of the University of Calcutta, and secondly to the eagerness with which the Brāhma Samāj welcomed this move on the part of the Government. The girls in the higher classes are practically all from the Brāhma Samāj, so much so that perhaps this influence is almost too predominant. A little Moslem girl who had received a special Government "stipend" on account of her religion, had recently turned Brāhmo, but the Head-mistress assured us that the change was due entirely to home influences. There is a good hostel in the school compound, for which there are always more applications than available vacancies, and arrangements are being made for the more complete separation of the school from the College department.

The function of the Inspectress is important,

and it is to be regretted that the word has come to suggest destructive rather than constructive criticism. "Training" is a more accurate description of the work, and in a country where a large proportion of the teachers are untrained, it well repays the money spent thereon. A visit often means three days spent in a village helping the teacher to a more scientific system. Suggestions as to improvements in the Code ought to come from the Inspectress, and she has every opportunity for studying the conditions of the people and the suitability of the type of education offered. To consider the relative value of European and Indian Inspectresses is at the present moment of purely theoretical interest. However great the advantage of the Indian in intimate knowledge of the environment and of the mental characteristics of the people, it is difficult as yet to procure any with the necessary scientific qualifications and gift of organization. The difficulties of travel are also accentuated for the Indian woman. The contribution of Indian thought should be in the meantime rather in the building up of individual schools, with ultimate constructive influence on the system as a whole.

The indigenous and spontaneous effort of the Indian community towards the education of their women is of two types, that of the Brāhma Samāj and reform societies, and that of the orthodox sections. The former is very much in line with the general system: the Code is used, and where alternative subjects are possible there is more emphasis laid on Sanskrit than in mission schools, but as a whole it is not strikingly "National." The Brāhma Girls' High School in Calcutta receives a monthly grant of five hundred Rupees and is a first class institution. Their Middle schools are mostly English in contrast to the vernacular mission schools. There are also a few Hindu Primary schools, which follow the Government Code. It is to the orthodox communities that we must turn to find the distinctively Indian note, the retention of which in any really educative scheme presents so baffling a problem. Here in the "Mahakali Pathshala" is a genuine Indian attempt at self-expression in educational ideals. This school was founded in 1393, in Calcutta, by "Her Holiness Mataji Maharani Tapaswini," one of those strange women saints who flit across the pages of Indian history, freed by their mystical insight and rare wisdom from the shackles of ordinary Indian womanhood. Hither the dainty little Hindu maiden of the upper castes is brought in a closed gari with her hands full of marigolds and other blossoms, to learn that school is but a larger home where the mysteries and ritual of worship will become clear to her, where she too will lisp the monotonous chant to the glory of the gods, and sink her baby soul in meditation. True, there is a printed curriculum on the wall, which says that Sanskrit, Bengali, Moral Text Books and Arithmetic are to be studied in six classes, but what matter! The effort which these subjects entail is ever and anon relieved by worship, and by the cooking which is part of worship. Then there is the picture of Saraswati Devi,[11] on whom "as the Wonder of all Wisdom one meditateth in the third watch of the night," and three hundred babies ranging from three to eight years of age will daily sway their little bodies before her in the morning *puja*.[12] What musical drill is in the Kindergarten so is *puja* to the Patshala pupils. There is a special prize for the best performer of *puja*—a sari and a silver pin for every little *Kumari*[13] who has honoured the school with her presence. The teachers are mostly elderly pandits, to whom the visit of the Inspectress indicates the desire of Government not to improve them, but to copy their most excellent methods in the Government schools! Regarded from a Western point of view the education is nil; the children can hardly read and write their own language, geography and arithmetic are practically absent, and there is no attempt to develop the mental faculties; from the point of view of the orthodox Hindu, however, it is probably ideal; the girls have "the ancient and sacred lore of their country infused into them and their lives are modelled after the ideal Hindu female characters of old." Herein lies the real value to the student of education: there is no gulf between

[11] The Goddess of Learning. On her festival, students will pile their books and inkpots before the shrines in their colleges for special blessing.

[12] Worship.

[13] Lady, a title of respect.

school and home, and the child's own environment and its hereditary instincts are utilized as a basis, but the trouble is that no superstructure is built thereon. Elsewhere we have superstructure but no basis. The school has no grant, no fees are paid, and the support is entirely obtained from subscriptions from the Hindu community. Extensively the influence of these schools is not great. There are nominally twenty-three branch schools in Bengal and Eastern Bengal, but a branch notified in the report is not always found to be in existence. That there is life in the movement is seen by the fact that the present Head, the Srimati Mataji, undertook a tour in the Mofussil and districts to organize branches. "She was everywhere well received, and there was evident sense of relief and sympathy of the public in the cause of female education under the Mahakali system."[14] To behold orthodox Hinduism sending a woman on tour in the interests of education is indeed to realise the Renaissance of the East! But "relief" from what? Is it from the non-religious character of the Government system?

The third and most potent factor in the educational situation is the missionary one. As this was the first in the field one would expect their work to be more highly developed, and it must also be remembered that the Brāhma Samāj is an indirect fruit of the leavening of Christian education. The doctrine of equal opportunity for man

[14] *Report of the Mahakali Patshala.*

and woman is seen at work in the comparative religious statistics of girls at school.

Primary .	5,360 Indian Christians to 126,897 Non-Christians.
Middle .	1,382 Indian Christians to 1,430 Non-Christians.
High .	448 Indian Christians to 667 Non-Christians.

As the returns of the Bengal census[15] show only 319,384 Christians in a total population of 52,668,269, these figures referring to their daughters' education are striking. The aim of Christian education is twofold, the building up of the Christian community so that ultimately the Indian Church may be a strong social factor, and the education of non-Christians with a view to influencing them either directly or indirectly in favour of Christianity. These two aims are combined in most mission work except in the case of most of the girls' Boarding schools where a non-Christian girl is naturally the exception. Of the eleven High schools for Indian girls in the Province, six are under mission management and two varying types may be noticed.

The Diocesan High school—a Government-aided institution for girls under the management of the Clewer Sisters, has the reputation of being the best girls' school in Calcutta. The reason for this is easy to discover in the personality of its Principal, Sister Mary Victoria, whose aristocratic idealism (if the words may be combined) determines the tone of

[15] 1911 Census. *Statistical Abstract of British India.*

the whole school. In India the personal element counts for everything, and without it, the best of institutions and Government plans are unavailing. Sister Mary Victoria and her English staff are constantly with the girls and when the school was first started they took their meals with the boarders until a tradition of manners was established. The school is well staffed with trained teachers both English and Indian, the former predominating. An English lady also who is interested in the school comes regularly to teach brushwork. There is an excellent College Department. The Government curriculum is followed, and in addition systematic religious instruction is given to all pupils. The ideal of this school is not, however, success in examinations only and their shadow does not lie heavily. As a small pupil remarked to the writer: "There are lots of girls in our school who don't love examinations, but who do love school." The pupils are drawn from various ranks and creeds; the boarders are mostly Christian, and the majority of the day scholars Hindu and Brāhma. The leading Indian families in Calcutta send their girls here, and to the Loretto Convent,[16] rather than to the Bethune School because of the personal contact with English ladies. The daily religious lesson is not felt as a deterrent in any way. It is curious to watch these girls drive up to the school in handsome carriages and to realize that they

[16] A school under the English Code, where only 15 per cent. of the pupils may be of Indian parentage.

are only paying two shillings and eight pence a month for a really first class education. Many of the richer parents give donations as well, but the fee is kept low for the sake of the poorer. These fees and the Government grant practically cover the working expenses of the school apart from the support of the English staff. There are no separate schools for the wealthier classes worked on a system of full payment, partly because poverty is not so much a cause of separation in India as in Britain and partly because there is not a sufficient number of girls ready for higher education who could and would pay fees that would cover expenses. Taken as a whole the fees in mission schools are higher than in Government institutions.

Of a somewhat different and more usual type is the United Free Church High school, it exists almost entirely for the girls of this and other missions who enter it as boarders from the country; the school is thus predominantly Christian and has little contact with Indian life. Of 122 scholars about 90 are boarders, and accommodation is being built for more. The day scholars are mostly in the lower classes. The education given is exceedingly thorough, and if the whole curriculum ending with a teachers' diploma is taken it ensures a girl a good post either in Government or mission service. There is no College Department, but a special feature since 1889 is the excellent Normal course from which most satisfactory results have been obtained. Miss Whyte may be rightly considered the pioneer of efficient training for teachers in Bengal. The Government curriculum is followed, and in addition the customary Biblical instruction is given. The school suffers from two drawbacks customary to all of its type, the lack of space and the "Westernization" of the pupils. Situated in one of the most crowded parts of the city, the buildings resemble a huge bee-hive packed with class rooms and dormitories and redeemed only by the glorious flat roof so characteristic of life in Calcutta. Below is a pathetically small playground where the boarders walk or read or play, in so far as the latter is natural to Indian girls. A splendid effort has been made by the staff to bring the girls into contact with nature and the historic monuments of India in order to counteract the cramping influence of the surroundings. One year a large party of teachers and former and present pupils visited Agra and Delhi, the wonder and glory of which opened a new field of thought and imagination to the Bengali girls. Another year the whole school was transferred for a short time to Deoghur. The material obtained on these expeditions served as a basis for nature study throughout the term. The students and elder girls are also taken once a year for a short mission tour, which serves not only to enlarge their horizon, but also emphasizes the primary purpose of the school. In spite, however, of the energy and originality of the staff in organizing these expeditions, the atmosphere of the school remains very much that of an ordinary secondary school in Scotland and has no distinctively Indian note. "Atmosphere" and curriculum are mutually dependent and their relationship is a problem that does not affect mission schools only. As a whole the mission High schools are doing a splendid work and their growing influence in the community is to be noted in the fact that occasionally Brāhma-Samāj and even Hindu girls are found amongst their boarders.

The Middle schools, teaching up to Standard V., have adopted the sound policy of excluding English, the object being to give a sound vernacular training to such children as will never have the chance of getting High school education. "It is these schools which supply the bulk of pupils to our training-schools for mistresses, and as such their importance in our system of female education in this country is very great."[17] The strong point of the mission schools, both Middle and Primary, is that they are under the direct and constant supervision of European workers. In one mission visited, all the Indian teachers were Christians and had had Normal training, and the schools were constantly visited by a lady holding the highest educational certificates. This is not the case everywhere, but it is the ideal aimed at. A mission Primary school is a pleasant place full of promise and of future possibilities. Shadow and sunshine are mingled, but on the whole the sunshine predominates. Take for example one in the vicinity of Calcutta

[17] *Bengal Public Instruction Report*, 1910.

Four Scholarship Girls. United Free Church Mission School for Hindus, Calcutta

—an old one-storied dwelling-house off a village lane, which skill has converted into a passable four-roomed school, with a sandy patch of ground used for drill and occasional geography lessons. There are about 120 children from five to eight years of age, the infant department is evidently looked upon as a sort of crêche by the village, for there are eighty babies sitting in solemn rows on the matting, but as soon as a girl becomes useful or marriageable she is withdrawn. Presiding over this happy family are three white-saried Christian girls, only one of whom has been trained as a teacher. The girl with the eighty pupils has only been as far as Standard III. herself; she is however making a loyal effort; the babies pass their wooden boards with very tidy hieroglyphics for inspection, but the impossiblity of it all makes one wonder if a Government grant is wisely given. The Head-mistress lends a kindly eye, but her attention is centred on Standard III. with its five select girls; this is the last year of Christian influences and these girls are being taught something not in the Government Code. They are bright and intelligent and the short Scripture lesson is enlivened by plenty of question and answer. Once a fortnight or once a week the school will be visited by an English lady, who will plan, supervise and if needful, give a model lesson. She has eight schools of this type under her personal superintendence, and her visits are the pivot on which they turn. A good Government grant is given;

the Code for vernacular Primary schools is followed, and as there is no competition the work is warmly welcomed by the Hindu community. The mission Primary schools hold their own in the educational system; of thirty-eight money prizes given by Government to Calcutta girls' Primary schools, all but three were won by mission pupils. The special characteristics of the missionary contribution to the educational problem, as a whole, are the presence of fully qualified European workers, who enter the educational sphere at salaries which no Government servant would accept, and the development of Normal work on scientific principles.

This review of the three agencies at work leads to the general consideration of some of the main problems which underlie the types and organization described, and which affect the educational outlook; the supply of teachers, the character of Secondary education, the development of Primary education and the co-ordination of the whole. The most crucial is undoubtedly that concerning the teacher.

The school career of the Bengali girl is limited at present in the large majority of cases to only four or five years, and there is thus no time for the teacher to waste. If education is to commend itself at all to the real India (as distinct from "Babudom") it must be of the very best type. The Government realize this and are putting forth every effort to procure trained teachers, but whence are the students to be obtained, and who is to train them? The unquestioned future for every Hindu and Moslem girl is matrimony and it is therefore only from amongst those who have been widowed in childhood that teachers can be drawn. But in spite of all that has been written and said on this subject the necessary education is still denied to them, by religion, custom, and prejudice. In the Hindu Female Training School in Calcutta, started by Government to surmount some of the initial prejudice in regard to the training of "*parda-nashin*" women, there are only seven pupils. They are all widows of above sixteen years and though they are not admitted unless, when children, they have been through the fourth standard, their brains have remained fallow for six years and the problem of their training is a difficult one. In the only other Government institution for non-Christians there are at present thirteen Moslems and nine Hindus, and many of them have to be taught reading and writing as well as the art of teaching. It will thus be seen that though the ultimate solution of the dearth of teachers may be found in the utilization of the young widows, public opinion will have to undergo a considerable change before it is possible.[18] From the Brāhma-Samāj community more is to be expected, and though the Brāhma-Samāj Training Class in Calcutta is not at present in a flourishing condition, they certainly contribute a fair proportion of teachers. It is, however, from the Christian community that

[18] *Cf.* Chap. VIII.

the teachers are chiefly drawn, and efforts are being made to secure their efficient training. Of the sixteen Training Institutions in Bengal thirteen are under mission management, and of 192 Indian pupils, 175 are Christian. A wholesome sign of the growing spirit of unity is the amalgamation of the training classes of four missions in Calcutta into one Christian Normal Training College with an excellent staff and a good modern equipment. So far it is only for mistresses who are to teach in the vernacular. Even with the large contribution of Christian teachers, the demand immensely exceeds the supply. Even before her examination there is hardly one of the candidates who has not secured a good post. They are in demand in the first instance for mission schools, in Brāhma-Samāj and non-sectarian institutions, and in Hindu and Model Primary schools. "The fact that they are Christians in a large number of cases is not considered a bar to their employment."[19] The inference for missionary societies is obvious—that to supply all the girls' schools of Bengal with teachers of strong Christian character would contribute much to the coming of the Kingdom of God. As regards the type of training given, the drawback is the fact that, like the Code, it is too Western. A solution may probably be found if the British educators are allowed to supplement their home-training by further studies on the spot, before undertaking work—a slower

[19] Inspectress's Report.

process but a surer one. Secondary training is yet to be developed both by missions and by Government. One Indian teacher has taken her degree of Bachelor of Teaching from a Mission school, but this is an isolated instance.

The relation of the statistics of Higher education to Primary is striking; only 11% of the girls at school are beyond the stage of just being able to read and write, while only 319 girls in the whole province are beyond the Middle stage. An immediate question is, How to retain the girls in the higher classes. Social and religious considerations weigh heavily here, as in the problem of the supply of teachers, but another influence may be, as elsewhere, the nature of the curriculum. This question has underlain much of the previous discussion, and is wide and far reaching in its scope. Indian education must have its own "Paradise"; the acme of Western civilization ought not to be reproduced in India, if diversity and not uniformity is the higher law. There is something lacking if the Mahakali committee speak of a "feeling of relief" in an escape from Government education, and some compromise is surely possible between their system and that of the Anglicized Boarding School. Destructive criticism is easy and there is plenty of it in Indian educational circles. On the one hand, the mission authorities say that they are bound by the hard and fast rules of the Code which conditions their grant, on the other, there is a great deal more liberality and elasticity in the Government policy than is commonly imagined, and a really well thought out curriculum on new lines would probably not mean the forfeiture of a grant. It is true that schools which vary from the type recognized at home are not aided by Government, but the Indian situation is different and it is probably for the good of the whole system that they should be under Government supervision and receive the impetus which comes from sharing in the educational scheme. Here is the opportunity for private enterprise and initiative; with co-operation on the part of the missionary societies in Calcutta it would surely be possible to remove one of their girls' High schools to the country and to give a practical demonstration of what modern education on Indian lines might mean. This would be no easy task and could only be accomplished by a staff who had intimately studied the conditions of Indian life and thought. This would be the most effectual "constructive criticism."

The extension of Primary education is a crucial problem throughout India; here in Bengal 95% of girls of school age are absolutely outside the educational pale. The wonder is, considering the inveterate indifference of the majority of parents and guardians to female education, even when it is freely given, that any progress is made at all. On the one hand there is the question whether it is advisable to encourage it too warmly, when the available supply of trained teachers is so disproportioned to the need; on the other, the

Standards I. to IV. United Free Church Mission School for Hindus, Calcutta

multiplication of schools and the acceptance of female education by public opinion would create a condition more favourable to the ready supply of teachers. The new Code for Primary schools introduced in 1910, which is in accord with modern educational principles, may prove more attractive than the former. Finance is an important matter. Many villages are too poor to maintain separate *pathshalas* for their daughters; there are at present 69,000 girls in boys' Primary schools as against 75,000 in Primary schools for girls only. The result is that in these villages the stricter castes do not send their girls to school and even the others are withdrawn after the infant stage. In the Secondary schools in the cities many girls who can well afford to pay are enjoying a first-class education for two shillings and eightpence a month at the expense of Government and missionary societies. This looks as if a re-adjustment of funds might increase the Primary statistics. Here again is an unlimited sphere for private enterprise; the mission school for girls only, staffed by Indian women teachers under European supervision is welcome and sure of success. The system of Zenana teaching both by missionaries and Government teachers is, as in Eastern Bengal, of great use in breaking down prejudice, and though apparently slow and costly work, it is invaluable.

It might possibly prove to be for the good of the whole system if some small central Board or consultative committee were formed to promote co-operation in the development of future plans between the Government and the various private enterprises.

The future of female education in Bengal is partly a question of administration, partly that of a greater number of European educators in sympathy with the genius of the country, partly that of a reformed curriculum, but more fundamentally it is a question of religious evolution.

VI

INTERESTING INSTITUTIONS IN THE UNITED PROVINCES AND PANJĀB

" The world exists in order to grow souls under the eyes of a patient, tireless, yearning Teacher."

From *Hindustan Review.*

IT is not proposed to give in this chapter a detailed account of general organization and of the forces at work. There is a definite similarity in the system of administration throughout all India, though it varies in its adaptation to indigenous institutions: one policy underlies missionary efforts, though they differ remarkably in the personal factor; the new Indian spirit is everywhere more or less articulate. But it is worth while to lay emphasis on certain phases of the problem of female education in the United Provinces, and on certain institutions in the Panjāb which are typical of the complexity of the situation, or present unique characteristics.

In the Quinquennial Survey the United Provinces occupy an unsatisfactory position at the bottom of the list of comparative percentages, showing only 1.2 per cent. of girls of school-going age at school. This percentage has, however, risen in 1910 to 1.33, and the total number of institutions has increased from 1,067 to 1,266—a creditable advance in the face of the difficulties to be encountered. The "impatient idealist" must beware, however, of extravagant hopes of transformation in a country where progress must of necessity be slow and of an evolutionary nature. Under more stringent inspection and regulation, the rapid advance in the early part of the decade has proved to a certain extent fictitious, and due to an over-hasty desire on the part of the educational authorities to move with the times. Local committees had apparently started schools for which there was no demand and for which they were unable to procure teachers. One Inspectress reports that in some cases, on a surprise visit, no teacher was found at all; in others, though the teachers were present, no work was being done.[1] Artificial efforts to hasten the pace were attended only by a spurious success; for example, a capitation grant of four annas a month was given in 1906 for every girl attending a boys' school, with a resulting increase of 4000 in the statistics of attendance; but a careful inspection and subsequent removal of the grant proved that the girls had simply been procured to sit in the schoolroom without receiving any attention, and that they left in a year or two as ignorant as when they entered it. Quite possibly some of the annas had found their way into the pockets of the parents who had been so obliging as to lend

[1] *Public Instruction Report, United Provinces*, 1910.

their girls. The latest statistics show a drop of 3000 in the total number of female scholars, but this is entirely among the girls attending boys' schools, and is due to the more efficient administration. The slight increase in the Secondary schools and in the girls' Primary schools is a sign of genuine progress and may be welcomed as such. The policy of the Government is one of slow advance after careful investigation and enlistment of local co-operation. About the year 1907, every District Officer was instructed to form a special committee to watch over the interests of girls' education in his district, and some of these committees have done excellent work, while others have been baffled by the difficulties to be faced and by lack of funds. Others, again, as indicated above, have tended to make haste too quickly. The fact that Indian non-Christian men of good social position have been found willing to serve on these committees is an indication of general advance and of growing sympathy with every effort for enlightenment and reform.[2]

As regards Inspectresses, the United Provinces are better staffed at present than any other province excepting possibly Madras, and yet the overwork is no less, for the districts are very large, and in many cases the schools are quite inaccessible to the woman traveller. But in a country where *parda* is strict, and where registers

[2] *Cf. Young India and the Education of Girls*, E. R. M'Neile (C.M.S.).

may only represent fictitious girls, and where moreover the work of the Inspectress is much needed for the stimulus and sympathy she can give, the system well repays the necessary expense, and will probably admit of yet further expansion. An effort is also being made to secure voluntary co-operation on the part of both English and Indian ladies who are willing and able to help. One Indian lady has given a great deal of her time to the inspection of the Government Primary schools in her district; another lady, a missionary with exceptional qualifications, is secretary of a local educational committee.

TABLE OF SCHOOLS FOR INDIAN GIRLS IN THE UNITED PROVINCES.[3]

Under Public Management.				Under Private Management.	
	Government.	Local or Municipal Branch.	Native States.	Aided.	Unaided.
High Schools	..	..	..	6	..
Middle— English	..	1	..	18	4
Vernacular	..	..	..	7	..
Primary	57	355	..	499	17
Training Schools	1	..	..	7	3
	58	356	..	537	24

[3] Formed from Statistical Tables III and IIIA. in *Public Instruction Report for United Provinces*, 1910.

The problem of finding teachers is even more acute here than elsewhere. It seems hardly credible that a teacher could be found in regular employment who was unable to write words of three letters to dictation, yet such is a recorded fact. Her ignorance had been concealed by a memorized knowledge of the Koran. Of sixty-two Primary schools sanctioned by Government in 1909 it has only been possible to open twenty-one because of the entire lack of teachers with even the minimum of qualification.

There are two lines of spontaneous Indian effort: the Ārya Samāj, whose schools conform to the Government Code and regulations, and neo-Hinduism,[4] which has produced Mrs Besant's school for Indian girls at Benares. The Ārya Samāj have a good training-school for teachers at Dehra Dun, students from which may be found teaching in their schools in other parts of India. A High-school department has recently been added to it, and every effort is being put forth to make it a strong educational centre. The school at Benares is in connexion with the Hindu Central College, and poses as a definite revolt from the anglicizing tendency of Government and mission schools. It receives no grant, and as yet has not even applied for inspection. The Government is considered to "favour Christian and mission schools," and therefore, though there is the same lack of funds here as elsewhere, the promoters will have none of it or its money! Freedom to

[4] *Cf. The Renaissance in India,* C. F. Andrews.

shape their own curriculum is also a dominant motive. To enter the school and see over a hundred beautifully dressed Indian girls, almost all of the Brahman caste, sitting in groups of six or seven, on bright carpets, the class-rooms well separated in the spacious airy building, was certainly to feel that here one might find a solution of the curriculum problem and a constructive theory of Indian education. "A training in conduct and religion is what Indians, as a rule, value most for their women—the work for those going beyond the rudiments is too bookish in character." [5] Here the teachers are free to saturate the instruction throughout with the ethical elements of a religion acceptable to the parents, to edit their own text-books, to emphasize the study of the vernaculars and Indian classics without the strain of examinations. The pupils stay longer than in other schools: many "married" girls of fifteen and sixteen years are in the upper forms. One particularly bright child of fourteen told us she was to be there for four years while her husband studied in England. Thus there is time really to influence the character and mind of the girls. Yet, on analysis, from the purely educational point of view the school was distinctly disappointing. As regards the staff, the Head-mistress, an English lady, claimed no knowledge of the vernacular, and though her intercourse with the girls seemed most cordial and sympathetic, it was necessarily limited, and

[5] *Public Instruction Report, United Provinces*, p. 34.

still more limited was her knowledge of their studies. An American with the degree of B.Sc., a Brahman, wife of one of the College professors, who had been educated in a convent, three mission-taught girls, and sundry other teachers of a nondescript character, completed the number. English was taught throughout, from class III. upwards, and used as a medium of instruction in classes VI. and VII., but the degree of fluency of the girls therein seemed hardly to justify this method. Many of the ordinary text-books were in use, and except for the moral catechisms and some stress laid on Indian art and Hinduism in the drawing lessons, the difference of the curriculum seemed more theoretical than actual. The theories are, however, suggestive, and when traced to the basal thought that education must be founded on the hereditary instinct and natural environment of the child they are not in reality revolutionary but compatible with the constructive system and ideals of the Christian religion.

The Crosthwaite High School at Allahabad shows possibilities of a different nature. It was started privately in Lucknow city some eighteen years ago by a committee of Indian gentlemen and Government officials, and was afterwards removed for the sake of a larger site and fresher air. A long, low, roomy building, with deep verandahs, forms the central school, with two hostels attached to it, in one of which twenty Moslem girls were residing, in the other six Hindus. A considerable number of day pupils, without restriction as to creed, are drawn from Allahabad. Tuition and conveyance for day pupils are given free, but the charge for boarders meets the cost. The Government Code is followed throughout, and the knowledge of English, tested by recitation and questioning on subject-matter, seemed of a thorough quality. The school illustrated in miniature most of the usual problems. It was marvellous that Moslem girls of really good family should have been allowed to come to a boarding-school, some from far distant States, and there was a certain pathos in the sight of them being taught by any kind of woman who had "learnt to read and write at home," and who in some cases might almost have been their ayah. This description applies only to the lower forms, but in these classes girls are at the most formative age, and many would not stay for the whole course. One teacher of this type was actually engaged in nursing her baby while giving an arithmetic lesson, and one wondered which of the two suffered more—the lesson or the baby! The Head-mistress was a young Indian Christian graduate from the Isabella Thoburn College, full of energy and enthusiasm for what seemed so difficult a task. She herself had to take three lessons a day, which left little leisure for the superintendence of the lower school with its double vernacular (Hindi and Urdu) standards throughout. A similar position in a school at home would have been occupied by a much older woman with many

The Isabella Thoburn College, Lucknow

years' experience of life. A question as to the religious teaching given elicited the following reply: "The Mohammedan teacher has her own girls; I teach the few Christians, and the Hindus look after their own bathings!" There is no question here of Indianizing the curriculum.

In turning to the specifically Christian institutions, it has again to be noted that the missionaries have been the pioneers of education, that an overwhelming proportion of the aided schools are under their management, and that a creditable proportion of Christian girls in the High stages (552 out of 759 Indian girls) is maintained. No account of women's education in India would be complete without a full description of the Isabella Thoburn College, or, as it is called throughout the Northern provinces, the "Lal Bagh" (Rose Garden). From a tiny beginning in 1870 as a bazaar school in Lucknow, with half a dozen Christian girls, it has grown by successive stages to a splendidly equipped collegiate institution, the portals of which may be entered by a child as a tiny "rosebud" for the Kindergarten, and from whence the full-blown B.A. may emerge some sixteen years later. The College and its latest additions stand as a memorial to two strong personalities, Isabella Thoburn, the founder, and Lilavati Singh, whose early death in 1909, when Vice-Principal of the College, removed one of the Indian leaders of women's education. The ideals after which they strove and the spirit of passionate sacrifice for others which dominated their lives form a strong tradition in the school. The American sense of community life which enters so markedly into their schools and colleges has been transferred with wise adaptation to the Indian environment; and the former pupils of the "Lal Bagh," scattered throughout India, are still under the glamour of their school days and are working out its inspiration. Self-government in all that regards the common interest is the rule of the College and Normal departments, and the same principle is being slowly established in the High school in the hope of developing the sense of responsibility so greatly needed in the Indian character. The girls are practically all Christian, but occasionally a non-Christian girl is found taking advantage of the splendid education which she could obtain nowhere else. The Zenana school, opened in 1909, is attended by some Hindu and Mohammedan girls desirous of a simple course with domestic science, and it is expected that this department will gradually increase. There is also a special hostel for Hindu or Mohammedan girls which has not yet been much utilized. The staff consists of seven or eight American graduates and about fifteen Indian teachers, some of whom are graduates also. There are no untrained teachers. This proportion in a school of some 200 pupils, and a College and Normal department of about 40, is refreshing after other institutions, but it in no way satisfies the standard of efficiency aimed at by the directors. The Normal department is of special importance, as teachers are supplied from it to all parts of Northern India. No student is admitted to the senior course who has not passed the Matriculation or equivalent examination, and the Government Report testifies to the thoroughness of the training given. A lower qualification is accepted for the Kindergarten course. The Government Code is followed throughout, and there is thus no question of an experimental curriculum on Indian lines. The College is under a Board of Directors which includes two prominent Indian gentlemen, and is in connexion with the American Methodist Mission.

The Church Missionary Society has an excellent boarding-school for Christian girls at Benares with about 100 pupils. The central schools for the Christian community form a very important part of the work of any mission, and it is entirely due to them that the creditable percentage of Christian girls in the Secondary stages is maintained. Where a Normal department can be added, their influence on the non-Christian community and on the general educational situation is very marked. Unfortunately some mission committees have still a tendency to appoint a pupil to a post too soon, and the numbers are not as large as they might be. The Benares class has at present nine students who entered it with Middle Anglo-Vernacular qualifications; its special feature, in addition to the ordinary subjects, is an experimental attempt to give some conception of the Hindu environment of religious thought to the students. The Indian Christian of the second or third generation tends to be totally isolated in idea and thought from other Indians, and this tendency is often accentuated in mission schools. It is therefore exceedingly important that those who are to influence Hindu life as teachers in mission or Government schools should, in the course of their training, form some clear and correct conception of the religious environment of their future pupils. Experimental work of this type should prove most useful in any future developments of Normal training which missionary societies may be contemplating.

There is throughout a pleasant spirit of co-operation between the various educational missionaries, and between them and the Government authorities. There is a Missionary Educational Union for the Province which the Inspectresses attend officially. An annual Teachers' Conference is held in February, and it is probable that in the future co-operation may pass from theory to actual fact in the development of further work. A striking lack in the missionary contribution is the absence of any school of really first-class character for non-Christian girls, such as exist in Bombay and Calcutta. The educational work for boys has been fully developed, but the parallel opportunity for girls which the changing times have created has yet to be seized. It may be argued that the Isabella Thoburn school has arrangements for non-Christian girls, but even in these changing times there are few non-Christians who would be willing to risk their daughters in a boarding-school among such an overwhelming number of Christian girls, whereas first-class schools starting fresh with no tradition would be sufficiently in touch with the new movement to attract pupils by their sheer efficiency. In this direction and in the training of teachers the standard must be set by the missionary authorities if their reputation as pioneers is to be maintained.

The situation in the Panjāb differs again only in degree. While there has been no ebb in the increasing tide of pupils—an increase of 1328 in 1909, and of 3732 in 1910, making a present total of over 42,000 girls under instruction—the problem of administration and inspection in a strictly *parda* country is as difficult as elsewhere, and there are stories of the inefficiency of the teachers which surpass even those told of other provinces. The municipalities vary greatly in their enthusiasm for the education of girls—Amritsar, for instance, being well supplied with thirty-five girls' schools, whereas Lahore has only one of this type. The missions have as elsewhere the system of boarding-schools for Christian girls, and carry on extensive work, chiefly of a Primary nature, among non-Christians of all races and creeds. Occasionally a non-Christian girl is found in a Christian boarding-school. Some of these schools are specially commended by the Inspectress for their teaching in domestic economy and sewing. " The Sialkot boarding-school divides the children into families of twelve girls who each do their own cooking, washing, and housework, even the little ones helping."[6] St Stephen's Girls' School (S. P. G.) has a special lace department where any girl who wishes to learn English may earn the money to pay the requisite fee. The lace produced is of a marketable quality, and not of the type which passes from bazaar to bazaar in Great Britain. The work of the Kinnaird Girls' High School, Lahore, is similar to that of the Bombay school[7] under the auspices of the same society (Z. B. M. M.). It is intended mainly for Indian Christian girls, but contains a certain proportion of others. The average age of leaving is about sixteen. Its training class is of special interest. Women students in the Panjāb are allowed to take the Junior Anglo-Vernacular training after matriculation, though, in the case of men the same examination is open only to graduates. In spite of this the girls generally stand fairly high in the lists, one of them recently taking the second place. The class, however, averages only some five students, though the school has over 160 girls. There is another excellent High school for Indian non-Christian girls in Lahore under the superintendence of an Indian Christian lady.

Here, too, slowly but surely, the voice of Young India is making itself heard in a new desire and a new effort. Lawyers, doctors, Government servants, are seeking for their wives and daughters

[6] *Public Instruction Report, Panjāb*, 1910.
[7] *Cf.* p. 178.

Church Missionary Society, Middle School, Amritsar.—Hoop Drill

an education which, if not equal to their own, will a least be a sufficient compromise between the old status and the new ideas to which they give utterance from public platforms and in the press. The reform sects, notably the Ārya Samāj, are ready with a definite educational policy of their own. They have a special orphanage at Ferozepore, and a considerable number of schools; the Dev Samāj, a new rallying-point, has two or more schools; there is a Sikh boarding-school near Amritsar; and, " in opposition to these reforming Hindu societies, at least one orthodox Hindu girls' school has been opened lately. Whether the activity of the reformers will force the orthodox Hindus to take an interest in girls' education and to start a network of schools in opposition remains to be seen." [8] The Maharani of Burdwar is noted for her efforts in this direction, and her schools, the Vedic Putri Pathshala and the Khatri Girls' School at Lahore, both aim at having High departments. Absolutely unique in its aim, management, and curriculum is the Victoria May Girls' High School, Lahore, now known as Queen Mary College. The idea of establishing a High school for Indian girls of good family was put forward by certain Indian ladies at the *parda* party held in honour of the visit of the then Princess of Wales in November 1905, and the possibility of putting this proposal into effect was

[8] *Female Education in North India. East and West,* January 1911. M. P. Western, Principal, Victoria May School.

attained by the munificence of certain leading Native States in the Panjāb. The school is under the management of five leading Indian gentlemen representing different creeds, and of two of the highest officials in the Province. Its curriculum is, so far as the writer's experience extends, the only one in which a definite constructive theory has been put forth for the education of Indian girls on such lines as combine excellent modern education with training suitable to their future environment.[9] Its ideals are defined in the following extract from the prospectus. "The proposed education is to be first and foremost womanly, therefore pupils will not be prepared for Matriculation until alternative courses of study suitable for girls be framed by the Education Department. The Indian ideals of self-sacrificing motherhood and simplicity of life will be held sacred, and the education given, while conducted on the best modern methods, seeks in every way to guard the ideal of the Indian wife in her home. For this reason the curriculum includes lessons on the care of children's health, simple remedies for ordinary illnesses, 'first aid,' invalid cookery, and science as applied to the home, in the shape of the elementary laws of sanitation, ventilation, etc." Great attention is paid to the vernaculars and to the beautiful

[9] The prospectus of the Conjeevaram School (South India) presents several unique features. The Hindus consider it their best school. A visit was, unfortunately, impossible.

Oriental scripts. Advanced pupils may study Persian or Sanskrit. A speciality is made of colloquial English, but there is no study of it as advanced literature. Moral instruction is given from the beautiful stories and poems of all religions, no sacred book being excluded, and is as effective as can be in an institution necessarily limited in its religious life and instruction. A great effort is being made to attract pupils from the families whose sons attend the Chiefs' College in Lahore; six or eight special suites of rooms are being reserved for rajahs' daughters and their necessary attendants, in new buildings attached to the Principal's house, and such facilities may do much to break down the barrier which has hitherto separated these classes from modern education. This school may serve not only as an inspiration to its actual pupils, but may have a reflex influence on the whole scheme of education. For instance, a course of lectures has recently been started in connection with it to demonstrate to Indian ladies the real needs of local girls' schools, and to induce them to act where possible as helpers and advisers. To turn what has hitherto proved an obstructive force into a definitely constructive one would surely be an excellent policy.

The Land of the Five Rivers has ever been a land of romance and of stirring life, and the modern movement for the enlightenment of its womankind has still the same elements, and is full of the promise of the future.

VII

SIDELIGHTS ON SOME NATIVE STATES

"Vulgarity is unknown in India. This alone is education and of the highest order. Reading and writing are minor to it."

From the *Indian Ladies' Magazine*.

TO the student of Indian problems the Native States present in many cases a survival of former conditions which elsewhere have been swept away under the more direct influence of British rule; in others freedom from the criticism to which an alien rule is liable has allowed advanced rulers to experiment on the most modern lines. The term "Native State" is itself capable of very diverse interpretation.[10] There are in all about seven hundred districts so called, with a total population of over 62 million, and varying in size from the great southern State of Hyderabad, with an area of over 82,000 square miles, to parcels of land about the size of an average country estate in England. The British Government takes direct cognizance of some hundred of these in varying degrees of relationship. Some States are entirely responsible

[10] *Administrative, Problems of British India*, book ii., chap. i. J. Chailley.

for their own internal government with a British Resident tactfully fulfilling his difficult office; in others the control is more direct, under an officer appointed as administrator by the Government till such time as the State finances or internal order may justify once more the revival of relative independence under an heir of the dynastic family. There is thus every variety of ruler, from the rajah who holds the time-honoured doctrine of "L'état c'est moi," and whose State recalls the prejudices, barbarities, and general practices of the Europe of the Middle Ages, to the virtuous chiefs who strive to rule on modern principles of order and justice for the welfare of their people. There are rajahs whose womenfolk are the strictest of *parda-nashin* and others whose daughters may disport themselves in English society at home to their hearts' content, a curious bye-product being the rani who is *parda-nashin* in her own State but not when she comes out into the world abroad.

It is natural that only amongst the more progressive States is any opportunity found of studying the question of female education; in others even the first beginnings are totally absent. The present chapter is in no sense a complete survey, and only offers a few notes which may indicate the general trend. It is difficult in many cases to obtain exact information, as the British Government are wisely chary of giving too much. The official reports, as M. Chailley puts it, wrap up blame in velvet and distribute praise with a liberal hand, and a letter to a native diwan[11] will not always procure an educational report with the same promptitude as it would in British territory. There is also the never-to-be-forgotten fact that "All the world's a stage," and at times the temptation to play a part, to produce a semblance of things which speak of progress and yet lack reality, is too strong for the Oriental mind. Thus a school housed in a magnificent building with four hundred girls on its roll may prove to have less than two hundred in daily attendance, though each child is in receipt of a monthly "stipend" from the State for the honour of her attendance; and "God save the Queen" may be cheerily sung in honour of the beloved Empress of whose death all India has not yet heard!

Some of the smaller Native States are closely linked educationally with the adjacent British province; the Inspectors visit them, and their statistics are included in the Provincial Report. Thus the Quinquennial Survey includes over 150,000 square miles of Native State territory, chiefly in the Bombay Presidency. In others, with which the Government of India maintains direct political relations, the educational policy depends entirely on the native ruler, and reflects his personality and enthusiasm. A very striking instance of this is Baroda, a small state with a population of about two million. A policy of stringent reform was inaugurated there about

[11] Chief minister.

1875, during the minority of the present Gaekwar, and has had its effect on the position of women. Two acts, legalizing the re-marriage of widows and raising the marriage age to twelve, have marked the tide of progress during the last decade. The educational movement dates from 1871, and there is now a complete system for boys from free Primary education to scholarships in Japanese Universities. The scheme for girls is less ambitious, but there are Primary schools in every village, teaching the ordinary curriculum up to Standard IV., a fair proportion of Secondary schools in which cooking is also taught by the teacher or by a Brahman cook, and a central High school in the capital with a Training college attached. Any girl of promise can secure a scholarship to it after the fourth or fifth Standard, and after a five years' course is certain of employment. The curriculum is very thorough, including astronomy, botany, mathematics, and the ordinary Normal course. There are at present about fifty students in the college, and a steadily increasing stream of applicants. My informant stated that there was no prejudice here against widows as teachers, and that even Brahman widows who were poorly off had entered the profession. The statistics are of special interest as showing the effect of compulsory education within a limited area. This experiment was introduced, for the first time in Indian history, in one district of Baroda in 1893, and was extended to the whole province in 1904. The age for girls is seven to ten, for boys from seven to twelve. The numbers in the girls' case rose from 9 % of school age at school in 1905 to 47% in 1910—an almost incredible rise in comparison with the slow movement in other parts of India. There is naturally a good deal to be said as to the wisdom of a policy which is so far in advance of the desire of the people. Some are said to be flying from Baroda into the adjacent British territory to escape what appears to them a meaningless tyranny.[12] The people are very poor and heavily taxed; they want the children to work, or to take charge of the other children while the women work in the fields. The richer parents, again, object to the girls leaving the house, as *parda* is fairly strict. There are pathetic tales of school-mistresses who, in addition to their scholastic duties, must start an hour and a half before the appointed time to compel unwilling feet into the path of knowledge, and stories of children who manage to arrive half an hour before the closing time in order to kindly swell the statistics of attendance. Then there is the usual prejudice against the unpractical nature of the curriculum, and its slavish similarity to the boys' course. But after all discounting of statistics and allowance for the undercurrent of revolt, there is evidently a good deal of honest educational work being done in Baroda, with some measure of success. There is even some talk of creating a Central Women's Department, where special needs might receive full consideration.

[12] *Public Instruction Report, Bombay*, 1910, p. 24.

One Inspectress, a Parsi lady, is at present working there, and assistants are shortly to be appointed.

In the great Mohammedan State of Hyderabad progress is naturally slower. Though the greater proportion of the inhabitants are Hindus, the Moslem influence, proceeding from the Nizam's Court, is the predominating one. The Wesleyan and American Baptist missions began pioneer work in the Primary education of girls about 1880, and have steadily developed it by tactful measures to higher stages. Effort on the part of the Government has been made only in recent years, and is not yet a very important factor, though the Nizam's *parda* school at the capital is the beginning of better things. In 1905 there were only 4467 girls under instruction out of a population of over eleven million ![13]

Mysore also owes its first movement towards female education to missionary influence. In 1840 the first mission school for girls was opened in Bangalore, and in 1868 the first Government school. As in other parts of India, girls are to be found in the *hobli* or local boys' school, but the usual difficulties prevent this method from being really effective. A great impulse was given to the whole enterprise not only in Mysore but in all southern India by the establishment, in 1881, of the Maharani's Girls' School in the capital. The Maharani has also taken a close personal interest in its progress. This school, raised to the

[13] *Imperial Gazetteer of India.*

dignity of a college, ranks as a first-class institution; its Head is a student from Newnham College, and the rest of the staff has proportional qualifications. The education is entirely free, but entrance at first was limited only to high-caste families, and its extension now to Christians and respectable girls of low caste is under various restrictions. As a result the college has done much to break the barrier which exists between high-caste women and education. The curriculum includes the Kindergarten stage and a department of domestic science. There are at present some 400 pupils, including many Brahman widows, who are being trained as teachers, and also some former pupils who return to complete their course, bringing their children with them. Besides this splendid effort in the capital, the Government has encouraged the formation of local committees for the development of education in the different districts. By 1904 there were 243 girls' schools and colleges, with a creditable percentage of four girls in the hundred at school. The London Missionary Society and others have extensive work here, and contribute considerably towards these statistics. Probably the most striking feature in the educational situation in Mysore is the introduction, in 1908, of definite religious teaching in the Government schools. This subject is more fully treated in a subsequent chapter.

Next to Baroda, the southern State of Travancore has the highest percentage of girls at school, namely, 23.3%. This is largely due to the fact that 31% of the population are Christians, and to the thorough work of the London Missionary Society; but the present Maharaj stands for educational reform, and an official effort is also made for the advancement of women. A somewhat similar impetus to that lent by the Maharani's College was given to the education of girls in Travancore by the establishment there of the Maharajah's College for girls under a fully qualified English Head-mistress, who has since been succeeded by an Indian lady. These two Indian institutions stand out beyond all others as examples of progressive native policy on wise lines.

The great group of Rajput States in the heart of which the British Government holds under its direct control the key lands of Ajmer-Merwara, have a history of romance and chivalry which might well have augured a leading place for their women in the modern movement, and yet it is just this very chivalry which shields them from its touch. The Rajput princesses of the ancient days were no pale, languishing maidens. They sallied forth armed and on horseback to lead a forlorn hope, or closed the gates of the castle against a lord who returned without the spoil of victory from the field. When the doom of their tribe was at hand and the Moslem hosts surged round the sacred city of Chitore, they passed in solemn procession to one common nuptial fire, while their lords perished in the wild holocaust of *johār*.[14] What wonder that, where the women were of this temper, their husbands and sons were able to defy all odds![15] Children of the sun and of the moon with all the glory of a mythic ancestry, the Rajputs have held apart from the seeming decadence of literary culture. True, there is the story of Jey Singh of the one hundred and nine virtues, whose mathematical calculations in the seventeenth century rank with those of European scholars, but he stands alone and reveals by contrast the prevalent conditions. The character of the rulers has thus in modern times influenced educational progress amongst their people, though only a very small percentage of these arc actually of Rajput descent. Alwar was the first State to move in 1842, and three years later Jaipur. It was not till some twenty years after that any official movement was made on behalf of women. The first girls' school was opened at Bharatpur in 1866,[16] but the progress has been very slow with little headway. In 1901 only two women out of every thousand could read. In 1905 there were, over the whole group of States, only fifty-three girls' schools, including the mission schools, and some of these were in a very poor state of efficiency. In Jaipur, which may be taken

[14] The great "war-sacrifice of honourable death" practised by the Rajputs. When resistance was unavailing, they chose death in battle rather than surrender.

[15] From *The Land of the Princes*, Gabrielle Festing.

[16] *Imperial Gazetteer*.

as the most advanced State educationally, the Government supports some eleven schools for girls. The principal one of these in the capital is supplied with splendid quarters. What money can do apart from personality has been done. The school, however, suffers most acutely from the prevailing difficulty of an inefficient staff. Some of the assistant teachers themselves are barely beyond the stage of being able to read and write, and thus the school as a whole lacks the attraction which is necessary to popularize education in a community where the hereditary tendency is against it. The marvel, however, is not that the school is not thoroughly modern, but that it is there at all; and if we remember the rapid strides which have been made in other parts of India from even smaller beginnings, it augurs well for the future of Jaipur. Mission-work in Native States depends greatly on the personal relations which the pioneers succeed in establishing with their rulers, and the United Free Church Mission has, since its first entrance in 1866 to the Native State of Rajputana, been exceedingly tactful in this matter. Its educational work for boys has been well developed and has helped very considerably in the general advance; on the women's side a great deal of careful pioneer work has been done by means of small schools and zenana visiting. There are at present sixteen of such schools with a total register of four hundred in six different States, also in Jaipur and elsewhere there is a considerable number of women under regular instruction in the zenanas. The efficiency of the schools varies according as they are more or less accessible to the regular visitation of an English lady worker. The work is entirely Primary as the *parda* custom is strict, and the children are withdrawn at about eight years of age.

The British District of Ajmer-Merwara does not, strictly speaking, fall within the purview of this chapter, but as it is essentially the key to all Rajasthan, its conditions have a reflex influence on the States, and the relation of the educational problems is a very vital one. The Government, while upholding the necessity of women's education, is greatly hampered in its efforts by financial considerations. The office of Inspectress, held since 1871 by a European lady educated in India, lapsed in 1892, and since then there has been no systematic effort to train teachers or effectually to supervise and co-ordinate the Government and independent schools. There are in all seven schools directly maintained by the Government, all of primitive type, quartered in rooms and courtyards rented in the bazaar, and of the 140 pupils only twelve are in the second Standard. The Government Report frankly acknowledges the inefficiency of these schools and urges the re-appointment of an Inspectress. The energies of the United Free Church Mission have been largely devoted in the past decade to the education of their famine orphans and the girls of the Christian community. Their Girls' Boarding-School in Nasirabad is a well-equipped

The Alphabet Class, Nasirabad

institution, and Normal work is under consideration. The tradition of Primary schools for non-Christians, since the first was founded in 1862, and of systematic zenana teaching, has been well maintained, and there are now about thirteen such with over four hundred pupils. There is, however, no really first-class education provided for the women of the non-Christian community, nor any attempt to meet the educational need of the changed times. The new spontaneous element is to be seen in the educational scheme of the Ārya Samāj, which has apparently a more religious aspect here than in other provinces. They have two schools for girls in Ajmer: one an orphanage with twenty-eight pupils under an honorary mistress; another, the Ārya Putri Pathshala, is an excellent vernacular Primary school with some provision for further instruction. The Head mistress is a fully trained teacher brought from another province, and the school throughout showed evidence of order and system. There are over sixty girls on the roll, and it seemed in every way the most efficient institution for non-Christians in the district. The most striking testimony to the new spirit and the new desire for progress was found in a private school conducted in her own house by the widow of a former leader of the Ārya community. It is true that in Ajmer the saying is still current that there cannot be two pens in one house, meaning thereby that to educate a girl is either to compass her own death or that of her future husband; but here some thirty-five girls, drawn not entirely from the Ārya Samāj but also from the leading orthodox castes, came daily at their own expense to get such learning as might help to fit them for life in its newer aspects. The Head-mistress, who had studied with her former husband, was a highly cultured Indian lady with a beautiful and attractive grace of manner, full of enthusiasm for her work, but almost pathetically conscious of the failure of her school to attain the ideals she had set before her. "I know geography ought to be taught but I cannot procure a teacher." "I have never even had an opportunity of learning English." "All my teachers teach for nothing; it is voluntary work, and education should not be otherwise." The school to a large extent reflected the personality of the Head. The attendance nearly equalled the number on the roll; far from reward being given, any children who did not come were fined for absence; several older girls were there, including some who were married, and whose husbands were away from home also studying. The school is strictly *parda*, for the Ārya community itself is only gradually advancing to freedom in this respect, and in any case the older pupils from the orthodox families would necessitate it. The education given is a thorough grounding in the Hindi and Urdu vernacular, with a limited amount of Sanskrit and careful instruction in needlework.

The whole situation in Ajmer, taken as an index to the future development of the States of

Rajasthan, points to the need for the establishment there of a first-class girls' school with an English Head-mistress to set the standard for the whole district, and this is strongly advocated in the Government Report, without, however, any prospect of immediate action. The class from which its pupils would be drawn would be at first a limited one, but its presence would to a certain extent increase the demand which is slowly but surely coming from men who realize the new need, and who know an efficient school when they see it.

This very inadequate survey of the conditions in some of the leading Native States will have served its purpose if the reader has gathered from it that the modern movement for the education of women is felt throughout the whole of our vast Indian Empire, varying in degree, but commending itself to the best Indian thought of every phase. It is not now a question of sporadic missionary effort or of a policy enforced by Government, but of a stream which is influencing the life of the people with an ever increasing momentum.

VIII

BOMBAY

"The true reformer has not to write on a clean slate. His work is more often to complete the half-written sentence."
—RANADE.

THE problem of women's education in the Bombay Presidency is to a certain extent that of the whole of India in miniature. Nothing is better calculated to impress the mind with the variety of races and social conditions, the conflicting ideals and different stages of progress throughout the whole Indian Empire, than a study of these in a smaller area at close quarters. Under the rule of the Governor are some 20,000,000 souls,[17] 75 % Hindus, 20 % Moslem, 1 % Jains, rather over 1 % Christians, and some 81,000 Parsis, whose social influence is out of all proportion to their numerical importance; a territory of 123,000 square miles, embracing the sun-beaten deserts of Sind, the fertile plains of Gujerat, the Deccan districts ever subject to the spectre of famine, the Carnatic regions with their glorious forests, and the low-lying tract below the

[17] *Statistical Abstract of British India*, 1911. Approximate figures.

Ghāts with its well-watered, broad reaches of alluvial soil—climates offering almost every variety of Indian possibilities except perhaps that of extreme cold. About a third of this territory belongs to Native States with a varying relation to the Presidency Government, and politically linked, though not strictly speaking attached, is the important State of Baroda with its 2,000,000 inhabitants. Linguistically considered, the province has four main languages, Marathi, Gujerati, Kanarese, and Hindi, with numerous linked dialects, and English will by no means take you everywhere, as some Anglophiles fondly imagine. Like all the rest of India it is a land of villages, only 19% of the people living in towns of more than 5000 inhabitants; a land of child-marriage, only 50% of the girl children under ten being unmarried, and a land therefore of young widows. These three facts involve a great difficulty in the distribution of schools, a brief curriculum, and a dearth of teachers. From a historical point of view the province presents stratum upon stratum; early records point to an Aryan settlement on the Indus amongst a people of Dravidian stock; Persian, Bactrian, and White Hun invasions have left their mark, but always the prevailing element is the Hindu—absorbing and Hinduizing the successive streams. The peaceful dominance of Asoka[2] is felt, and the Buddhist establishments whose records are left

Asoka, ruler of India, B.C. 272-231. He is known as the Constantine of Buddhism.

in the rock caves and temples must have been numerous and far-reaching. There are tales of chiefs who honoured alike Siva, Buddha, and Jaina In the seventh century A.D. trade brought the Parsis, a people of a book and a faith which still preserves them as a unity. In the eighth century came the first wave of the Moslem tide which was destined in later centuries to overrun the Deccan. In the fifteenth century came the Portuguese in search of "spices and Christians"; there are caves to-day where the ruins of Catholic altars lie side by side with Buddhist semi-reliefs, mingled with the ever-present Hindu forms and figures. The romance of the province, however, lies in the history of the Mahrattas, whose forts dominate the frowning eminences of the Ghāts, memorials of the gradual consolidation of the scattered Hindu chieftains, of prolonged struggle with Delhi, of internal strife, of defeat, of victory, until finally a new power from the West came to impose the dominance of the Pax Britannica upon the conflicting forces. The Presidency assumed something like its present form between 1803 and 1827, and the history of Western education may be said to begin with Mountstuart Elphinstone (1819-1827), in whose Governorship the first schools were opened.

The same factors which we found to be present elsewhere, working in favour of female education or against it, are felt in the Bombay Presidency. In some places, especially in the country districts, there is strong opposition to the establishment of any kind of schools at all, and most of all to girls' schools. To the zemindar or villager the establishment of a school merely means that educational and revenue officers will come round worrying him to support it. The children are wanted for work in the fields, and where the margin of subsistence is so small it is no wonder that every mite of labour is needed. In sixty villages out of every hundred there is no school at all. The women are conservative; they have not been educated themselves: why should their daughters be educated? Above all it is not *dustūr* (custom), and with that the would-be recruiting agency strikes against a solid argument which it will take decades to remove. But to set against this, there is the fact that, speaking broadly, it is not a *parda* country. Except for the Moslems, who are in considerable minority, and a small proportion of the Hindus influenced by tradition and contact with Mohammedanism, especially in the district of Sind, the women of both high and low caste have a certain degree of freedom, and their general position is greatly influenced by the presence of the Parsi ladies, who mingle in society very much as do their sisters of the West. To see an Indian lady walking on the streets of Bombay is no strange sight, as it still is in Calcutta, in spite of the half-shy efforts of Christian and Brāhma Samāj women. The indigenous Indian feeling in favour of education is stronger than in the district round Calcutta, and there is more of the orthodox element in it. Poona, the centre of the Deccan Brahmans and of cultured Hinduism, stands for a certain well-defined attitude towards education in which women share. The Prabhu Brahmans especially are noted for the many cultured women in their ranks; they do not marry young, and as a rule afford almost equal opportunity to boys and girls. The Prārthanā Samāj,[3] an unorthodox meeting-ground for the "multitudes in the valley of decision," throws its emphasis on women's education, and the general impression given is that, while all educated India has talked about this crucial problem, here much honest effort has been made to solve it. It is a very pure form of patriotism which leads a Hindu student to give up two hours daily of his college time to voluntary teaching in a girls' High school, yet this is by no means rare in Bombay. The Parsi element and influence has also been a very potent one. The leading Parsi men in the early days spared neither money nor personal trouble, with the result that to-day out of 1465 girls receiving higher education, 1054 are drawn from the Parsi community, and their contribution to the supply of teachers is a very important one.

But this leads us to a detailed study of the early history of the movement, and its present conditions in relation to the different communities.

[3] A society similar to the Brāhma Samāj, but less organized and not so strong numerically. *Cf. New Ideas in India.* Morrison.

Owing to the influences described, it is not surprising that, at the last Quinquennial Survey, Bombay stood second only to Burma in its percentage of girls at school, and a glance at the gradually increasing number shows the steady upward progress.

1881—1.2	per cent.	of girls	of school age	at school.
1896—3.75	,,	,,	,,	,,
1901—4.74	,,	,,	,,	,,
1907—5.9	,,	,,	,,	,,
1910—7.2	,,	,,	,,	,,

In earlier days it is impossible to get separate figures. Where girls shared in education it was incidentally in the boys' schools, or separately in mission schools, and they owed nothing to any special effort on their behalf; even to day 21% of the girls at school are studying in boys' schools. The initial impulse came from Mrs Margaret Wilson and other workers of the Scottish Mission, who from 1824 onwards gradually gathered together a few girls for instruction. The first step taken by Indians was due to the Students' Literary and Scientific Society connected with the Elphinstone College in Bombay, when five leading Indian members volunteered in 1849 to open schools for girls in their own houses. One of these was Mr Dadabhai Nauraji, India's "Grand Old Man," who may be regarded as the pioneer of women's education in the Presidency, if not in all India, and who still, in his eighty-sixth year, advocates their cause by his pen. A description of the celebrations in honour of his birthday organized recently by the "Gujerati Stri Mandal," a women's society founded in 1909 to further the educational and social progress of women, may give some idea of the distance which has been traversed since these early days. Some thousand women in their graceful Indian dresses, diaphanous draperies and brilliant jewels, gathered together in a hall which they themselves had garlanded and cross-garlanded with sweet-scented wreaths in his honour, while on the platform the Rani of Gondal presided, surrounded by all the leading Indian women in Bombay who were interested, either as organizers or teachers, in women's education. A short, terse speech was made by Miss Cursetji, whose main interest and energy for the last twenty-five years have been devoted to the Alexandra Girls' High School, founded by her father in 1863; another by the Hindu Head-mistress of the High School under the auspices of the Scientific and Literary Society; another by a young Parsi B.A., Head mistress of the first Hindu Girls' High School; another, in the general interests of education, by a Saraswat Brahman lady, whose husband is Prime Minister in an adjacent Native State—and the one European member of the audience realized that India has initiative and purpose of her own, and women of whom she may well be proud. The progress in the different communities and the share which is borne by the Government and private efforts respectively can best be seen by the accompanying tables. Private effort divides itself naturally, as elsewhère, into the work of Christian missions and of the Indian community, but a further sub-division is necessary in the latter in consequence of the special position of the Parsis.

Of the Hindu effort first :—the Scientific and Literary Society, after its initial private efforts, proceeded with a definite educational policy in the founding of schools, and, though at present only one school in Bombay is directly under its auspices, its influence in combating prejudice is considerable. This school is exceedingly popular, as the girls are passed quickly into the higher stages, thus earning a certain matrimonial prestige, though it is unfortunately true that a girl from the Matriculation class on transference to a mission school had to be placed three classes lower to find her proper level. In consequence of the amateur staff of voluntary teachers who supply the upper forms, this school does not rank as one of the eleven High schools. This feature is interesting, as it shows the earnestness of purpose in the members of the Society, but from an educational point of view the system does not seem very effective. As a whole the school presents no specially Indian features, except that French is excluded and Sanskrit is compulsory as a Matriculation subject. Religion is taught by a special teacher, and there are daily prayers. One Hindu school in Poona ranks as a genuine High school, and one other in Bombay hopes shortly to be classed as such. This Chanda-Ramji School owes its foundation to a legacy left for the build-

1909-1910

TABLE OF SCHOOLS FOR INDIAN GIRLS IN BOMBAY PRESIDENCY

	UNDER PUBLIC MANAGEMENT.			UNDER PRIVATE MANAGEMENT.	
Type of School.	Government.	District or Municipal Board.	Native State.	Aided.	Unaided.
High Schools	2	..	..	9	2
Middle [4]—					
English	..	1	2	30	4
Vernacular	..	..	..	..	..
Primary [5]	6	573	249	257	19
Training Schools	4	1	1	5	2
	12	575	252	301	27

This Table has been formed by the subtraction of the Anglo-Indian schools from Statistical Table III., *Public Instruction Report, Bombay Presidency*, 1910.

[4] There are also 190 girls studying in the High Stage of 12 of the schools classified for various reasons as Middle.

[5] High and Middle schools which have a Primary Department are included again in the returns of Primary schools.

TABLE SHOWING RACE OR CREED [6]

Type of School.	Eurasians.	Native Christians.	Brahmans.	Non-Brahman Hindus.	Moslems.	Parsis.	Others.
Primary . . .	4	2,905	15,329	42,185	10,077	3,934	492
Middle . . .	636	1,656	74	447	15	252	31
High . . .	1,492	151	107	77	42	1,095	86
Training Colleges . .	16	83	97	115	21	2	11
	2,148	4,795	15,607	42,824	10,155	5,283	620

[6] *Public Instruction Report, Bombay*, Table IIIA.

ing of a huge gilded idol. The idol was indeed built, but the times have advanced, and only some 10% of the funds were thus utilized. The school is excellently staffed with fourteen mistresses, four of whom are graduates, and with additional pandits for Sanskrit and mathematics for some two hundred girls; there is a splendid hall for drill and games, a well-stocked science museum, and practically every modern apparatus. Religion is taught from a book of Hindu Moral Maxims by a special teacher. The Gujerati Stri Mandal, mentioned above, has its own functions in endeavouring to secure the attendance at its afternoon classes of young married girls and others from the *parda*-keeping sections. Educationally, their influence is probably important rather in the direction of making the next generation accessible to proper education than in much actual attainment on the part of the present pupils. They also organize regular lectures on such subjects as "The Aim of Life," "The Advantages of a Spiritual Temperament," and "The Duties of Motherhood," from which may be seen the close connexion in the mind of the Indian woman between religion and education. The Prārthanā Samāj, though they have a weekly women's meeting for the discussion of ethical subjects, and a "Sunday School," do not organize any separate secular education, and their girls are to be found wherever the best education seems obtainable. In Hyderabad there are five large girls' Primary schools, managed by the Hindu

Reform Association, which the Government Report notes as doing useful work. It will thus be seen that the actual Hindu contribution to organized education is not an extensive one, nor has it, as in Bengal, any special characteristic; but it should be borne in mind that the Hindus take good advantage of the mission and Government schools, and are even found in some of the Parsi High schools. Though their percentage of girls in the High school stage is small in comparison with their overwhelming majority in the community, it is probably true that every orthodox girl venturing to continue her school career beyond the Primary classes, does so in spite of the opposition, if not of her own immediate family, at least of her grandmother and cousins.

The Mohammedan factor is numerically a small one; the girls belonging to families of the better class are educated at home or in one of the mission "English teaching"[7] schools, and it is interesting to note one Mohammedan lady of good social position guiding a school for poor Moslem girls in her own house. Two Mohammedan schools are also on the Government list of Primary schools, but the pupils are mostly in the lower Primary stage.

The Parsi contribution is, as has already been indicated, a very considerable one, and in its extent, thoroughness, and modern character, it is

[7] "English-teaching" schools form a special category in the Bombay Presidency. There is no limitation to the number of Indian pupils, and they are not bound by the Anglo-Vernacular Code. *Cf.* p. 179.

quite what one might have expected of the "French of the East." A few notes on their general position are needed to show their attitude towards education. The Parsis are one of the most adaptable races of the world, and in Bombay, where 46,000 of them reside, they have been the leaders in women's education. Lady Frere speaks of a time in her remembrance when not a single Parsi lady could speak English, whereas to-day it is almost as much a common tongue among the wealthy families as Gujerati, which they adopted on their original immigration to India. In 1842 Lady Arthur opened Government House for the first time to Indian ladies, and the Parsis were naturally the first to respond. To-day all the larger social functions in Bombay are attended by Indian ladies, the large majority of whom are Parsi.[8] They are to be seen daily at the Princess Mary Gymkhana, a ladies' club, playing Badminton and croquet, and discussing matters of interest with their friends, some wearing the orthodox *sari* and sacred shirt symbolic of their ancient faith, others in modern European dress. Socially they have been much affected by the hedonism of the West. Religiously their evolution has been rather negative than positive. Zoroastrianism as a cult had survived only in curious forms and ceremonies, and the sacred language of its books was unknown even to the priests; the educated Parsi inclined to agnosticism or theosophy while retaining his ceremonial adherence to a religion

[8] Hindu ladies attended first about 1863 in response to special efforts made on their behalf by Lady Frere.

which was the binding tie of his community. Under the influence of the modern Renaissance and general revival of the ethnic faiths, the sacred books have been translated ; brief extracts published in dainty vellum volumes, together with the Lord's Prayer and Christian hymns (with significant omissions), are used as manuals of devotion. When the Parsi girls' schools were first started no religious instruction was given, but now a special Zoroastrian committee exists for preparing literature and sending an instructor to each. Quick to perceive the general bearing of British rule and modern education on their position as a wealthy minority in an alien land, the Parsi leaders adopted, in 1857, a definite educational policy for their women. They separated from the Scientific and Literary Society and formed one of their own, the Parsi School Association, to which they gave most liberally both in money and personal service. Other leading Parsis founded special schools, and it is difficult when looking down the Government list to know which to select for description. Two perhaps may be taken as typical, one of the three Association schools and the Alexandra Native Girls' High School. The former owes its special characteristics to the Honorary Secretary of the Association, Khan Bahadur Chichgar, who visited the best schools in Europe in order to study the Herbartian principles of education in actual practice. He was the first to introduce this method in the Bombay Presidency, and has done so without imitation of detail, and with the most wonderful adaptation to the environment of Parsi children. The school is kept continually supplied with the latest appliances and the newest books, and Mr Chichgar has for many years visited the school on Saturday afternoons to train the teachers in the use of them. The result is that, though the teachers may hold no Normal certificates, the school is alert and keen, from the youngest baby rejoicing in plaiting its neighbour's hair, to the girls of the fifth form, whose curriculum is varied by ambulance work, cooking, and dress-cutting. On the occasion of the writer's visit every child had some practical handwork of its own to exhibit; the action songs were definitely related to the subsequent lesson on weights and measures, while the mud modelling of the Bombay water-system done by one of the higher forms showed a thorough sense of neatness and proportion, with an intelligent knowledge of the principle involved. The shadow of an examination never falls upon this school; it aims at providing a thorough training for life for middle-class Parsi girls, and its success in doing so in entirely due to the unsparing devotion and labour given to it by its founder—a man engaged in ordinary business.

The Alexandra Native Girls' High School dates from the early days of pioneer work and of unsympathetic criticism. Some 20 pupils were registered for its first opening in 1863, and to-day there are about 120, practically as many as the staff of the institution is meant to deal with. Its aim is to give Parsi girls of respectable families the "blessings of an English education upon sound moral principles," and though the blessing may be a doubtful one, the school is certainly thoroughly English in every way. Since 1890, Matriculation candidates have been sent up with a good record of success. There is no higher teaching of the vernaculars, and French is taken as the alternative Matriculation subject. The Head-mistress is from England and is fully qualified, but the rest of the staff are Parsis, only one of whom had Normal qualifications. The school is managed by a committee of leading Parsis, and though it is under Government inspection it receives no grant, as the income from fees and the endowment is sufficient. This school may be taken as fairly typical of a first-class Parsi High school. Moreover, education has advanced so far in the community that private enterprise is no longer an impossiblity, and can even as in the case of the Girton High school, be made financially successful without the Government grant. The dividing line between business and philanthropy may at times be difficult to draw, but the spirit is much to be commended which keeps a school of this type alive and efficient, when in some cases the nett profit to the proprietress is barely a living wage. Taken as a whole, the Parsis have provided most thoroughly for the education of their girls, both rich and poor. Of the eleven High schools under private management in the Presidency, seven are Parsi; of the Middle schools four, and of the Primary schools, whether separate or forming departments of the High schools, fifteen. Of this provision ample advantage is taken, and the proportion of daily attendance to the numbers on the roll is amazing in comparison with Upper India.

Wherein, then, does the system fail, or is it perfect? Criticism seems ungracious where so much energy and thought have been expended, but in the main there are two things which strike a visitor—the lack in the teachers of a sense of the dignity and responsibility of their profession, with the consequent effect of such a lack on the outlook of their pupils, and the de-orientalizing curriculum. These problems are, however, common to the whole educational situation, and one could hardly expect even the Parsi community to be quite immune.

It is difficult to turn from the indigenous Indian element, which has naturally something in it very spectacular and attractive to the Western visitor, to the quiet record of the immense and steady contribution of Christian missions to education in the Bombay Presidency, and to realize that the main inspiration of the former came from the gradual and unconscious infiltration of the Christian ideal of womanhood. For more than twenty years the missionaries were the sole pioneers in the face of much opposition. The pupils were gained at first through the influence of Hindu and Parsi gentlemen interested in the Scottish mission. Progress was naturally slow, there was a lack of continuity in the British workers, and continuity is essential in a country where personality counts for so much; but by 1827 three hundred girls, some of good caste, were attending school in the Konkan district, where the Scottish pioneers first started. After the transference of the mission Mrs Wilson had managed, by 1830, to organize six little schools in Bombay with 120 pupils, the story of the winning of each individual girl being almost a romance in itself. For some time the children were given weekly *paisa*[9] as a reward, and would demand their wage like weary labourers, a practice still extant in some of the Native States, and a great contrast to the sum of 407 rupees now received as fees in one of the mission institutions which traces its origin to these very schools. The Parsis in one street asked the mission to instruct all the children therein, including sixteen girls. The Beni Israel also proved an accessible community, and thus gradually the number of girls increased. The second stage of missionary education was reached when boarding-schools were created for Indian Christian girls who could be retained for a reasonable time, and some of whom could be utilized as teachers. About 1885 the first systematic attempt at Normal training is noticed, a line of work which is perhaps at present the most important missionary contribution to the whole scheme, and capable of further development. Mission schools, as might be expected, form an

[9] Farthings.

overwhelming majority in the list of aided schools. Of the 11 High schools they have 2, of the 34 Middle schools 14, and of the 276 Primary schools, practically all except those indicated above and a few others. Certain societies educate, as yet, mainly the children of their own communities; others, such as the American Board for Foreign Missions, the United Free Church of Scotland, and the Irish Presbyterian Mission, have a considerable number of schools, both in the cities and in the villages, for non-Christian children. The Zenana Bible and Medical Mission makes work of this kind a special feature.[10] The small proportion of High schools is partly accounted for by the fact that the Victoria High School at Poona, founded by Mrs Sorabji, and still carried on most effectively by her daughter as a Christian school, is classed as a boys' school. It is attended by the children of many of the leading Parsi families, and is a curious example of successful co-education up to an advanced stage. Also both in Bombay and Poona there is a considerable number of good European schools in connection with Roman Catholic and Episcopal sisterhoods, to which 15% of Indian girls may be admitted on payment of double fees. These places are always eagerly sought. The Girgaum High School, under the auspices of the Z.B.M.M.,

[10] Detailed information can be obtained in the reports of the various societies. There are 26 Protestant societies in the Presidency, most of whom have educational work for girls.

may be taken as typical of a first-class "English-teaching" mission High school. About 150 girls can be seen gathered together at morning prayer, two-thirds of whom are non-Christian (Parsis, Moslems, Beni Israel, and a few Hindus); some have come in their motor-cars, others from quite poor homes. The curriculum extends from three Kindergarten classes to the seventh English standard, in which the girls go up for Matriculation. English is used as a medium throughout, which makes the school popular with Indians who desire purely English education, but it is naturally very difficult for the pupils in the early stages, in spite of the Government regulation that the teacher must be able to translate into Marathi. There are four English mistresses and several well-qualified Anglo-Indians. A new department has recently been added for the training of English Kindergarten students for the Froebel examination, but this is not yet sufficiently staffed to ensure good success. Two-thirds of the income are derived from fees and one-third from the Government grant.

The Ambroli School of the United Free Church Mission is Hindu throughout, and at present takes its pupils only as far as the fifth Anglo-Vernacular standard. All the instruction in the lower forms is in Marathi, and it is a stiff battle that Marathi babies have to fight with their letters. There are three scripts to learn—one printed, one cursive, and one abbreviated—and it is no wonder that, with this task to master, Indian parents tend to look on Kindergarten expedients for "time wasting " as a diversion from the royal road to knowledge. The teachers here, with the exception of one Anglo-Indian for English in the upper forms, are all Indian, and some are non-Christians, but the school is continually visited by a fully trained Scottish lady, who divides her time between this and another school. Fees are paid regularly, and there is a good municipal grant. An interesting feature of the American Mission is the stress laid at their orphanage and boarding-school upon independence in character. Each pupil must do two hours' industrial work, and may in addition work longer for payment, which is credited to her account for payment of fees. Thus some of the pupils in the Matriculation class were beyond the usual age, but had contributed considerably to their own maintenance. The industrial training of this mission is very highly developed, both in Bombay and at Ahmednagar. The Primary schools in the villages have the usual characteristics which we have studied elsewhere, and it has only to be noted that this work is capable of practically unlimited extension.

No account of women's education in the Presidency would be complete without reference to the work of Pandita Ramabai,[11] which stands outside all mission control, and is the unique contribution of an Indian woman to the future victory of the Christian ideal among her own people. Since the *Sharada Sadan* (the abode of wisdom) near Poona was started in 1892, thou-

[11] *Cf. Life of Pandita Ramabai*, Helen Dyer.

sands of Indian widows have been given the opportinuty of a self-supporting, self-respecting life, and a vision of what self-sacrifice may mean. The education given on strictly intellectual lines is naturally not carried to a High stage, but is thorough in type. The Pandita dreads the Westernization of her girls, and stands for all that is good in simple Indian life.

Though mission education bulks so largely in the statistics of voluntary schools, and has been the pioneer, it must be realized that it does *not* hold the same position in this as in other provinces, nor influence the districts as a whole. A brief glance at the figures of Primary schools (Table, page 168) supported by other public bodies, both in British territory and in the Native States, will prove the contrary to those who imagine the mission factor still to be the dominant one.

The Government function is here, as in the other provinces, largely a co-ordinating and directing one as regards the girls' schools. The six important Government institutions—two High schools with Primary schools attached, at Poona and at Ahmedabad, and four Training schools—are a direct outcome of the effort to standardize and raise the general tone of education in the Presidency. They are linked by the system of "stipends" to all the Primary schools. The institution at Poona under an Indian lady, Miss Bhore, is excellently housed, and had at the time of my visit 200 girls in the High school, 200 in the vernacular practising school, and about 88

Normal students. The Inspectress regrets that there is not a Government High school in Bombay to raise the general standard. Apart from these institutions directly under the Central authority, a great deal has been done with public funds under the Municipalities and Local Boards. It has been impossible to ascertain exactly when these schools under public authority were first started, but the system must have grown up somewhere in the "eighties." At first the girls of the lower castes went, as they still go in many villages, to the boys' schools; in other places separate schools gradually sprang up wherever there were enlightened Indian members of the Municipalities to welcome the official suggestion. In 1901, the number of girls' Primary schools in Bombay necessitated the appointment of an Indian Inspectress to work under the Municipality, and shortly afterwards an English Inspectress was appointed from home to the Indian Educational Service, in order to develop women's education in certain portions of the Presidency. Her time was largely occupied in the inspection and examination of Training colleges and High schools (European and Anglo-Vernacular) and in dealing with questions of general educational policy as "expert adviser" to the Department. Since Miss Ashworth's retirement, no English Inspectress has been appointed in the Indian Educational Service to this Presidency. The value of the municipal and local board schools, if viewed from the numerical standpoint of increasing the women literates in the district, is unquestioned, but when all allowance has been made for exceptions, the real gain to the community when the schools are not well staffed and lack constant supervision is very questionable. Miss Corkery, the present Inspectress, emphasizes the need for constant inspection. "I believe that if the Municipalities employed a trained supervisor to visit each school daily the work would be carried on more methodically. From my twenty-five years' experience of the Hindu female teacher I have come to the conclusion that she has no power of initiative and no administrative capacity. She will work hard and faithfully under supervision, but as soon as that is withdrawn her natural apathy asserts itself."[12] When in addition to her own "natural apathy" the teacher has possibly had no Normal training herself, and suffers from untrained assistants, the spirit of the school is apt to flag. Adequate inspection of these schools would undoubtedly necessitate the appointment of women Deputy-Inspectors. The question of premises is also a very vital one. The Indian child is accustomed to be one of a crowd, to eat and sleep, to live and die as one of a crowd; but, in school, if it is to attain to individuality, it must learn the value of space. Yet in one of the best Bombay municipal schools which takes its brighter pupils up to the Anglo-Vernacular sixth Standard, I found some 300 girls crowded into the space

[12] *Public Instruction Report, Bombay*, 1910, p. 27.

really needed for about half that number. Several crowded pens were to be seen round a bit of flat roof, too wet in the rains and too sunny at other times for drill, one of the pens so crammed with infants that it was almost impossible to step from one division to another, infants in different classes within touch of one another, and the whole pervaded with a pungent odour from the fruit market below—surely this is not for the good of the city or of the children. "In Ahmedabad the girls are compelled to sit amid insanitary and evil-smelling surroundings, to study the advantages of pure air."[13] It would not be difficult to multiply instances. On the other hand some municipal schools are well housed and staffed, and the system must not be condemned when it is capable of improvement. The problem is partly a financial one, and partly once more the question of the supply of teachers and of the future Inspectresses. These children pay a few *paisa*, in fair proportion to the income of their parents, whereas in many High schools receiving a Government grant the fees might with advantage be raised.[14]

When the situation in the Presidency is viewed as a whole the present need is seen to be not so much to secure more girls by artificial means or to induce more to stay to the higher stage, for there is a steady current in favour of education which is slowly acquiring momentum, but rather to raise the standard of teaching as a whole and

[13] *Public Instruction Report, Bombay*, p. 27.
[14] *Ibid.*, p. 18.

so to adapt the curriculum that those children who do pass through the schools will, in intellectual attainment and character, commend the system and prove a force attractive to others.

The problem of the teacher is one that is apparent throughout, alike in Indian, mission, and public authority schools. Taking the Primary teacher first, from what ranks is she usually drawn, and what are the attractions to the profession? In consequence of the shortness of supply the schoolmistress is very often found to be, in fact, an elderly man. This, however, is becoming less frequent. A glance at the table on page 168 shows that the majority of students in training are lower-caste Hindus, and that native Christians form about a fourth of the whole. Of the 1200 women actually engaged now in the teaching profession, I have been unable to obtain a religious classification, but presumably the proportion holds good. In the Ahmedabad Training College 15 of the students are wives or daughters of masters, 19 are wives of students, 15 are wives of other men, 42 are unmarried, and 36 are widows. Taking this college as typical, and assuming the certainty of marriage on the part of the spinsters, it means that in many cases teachers will be available in couples for the village schools. Those whose husbands are not teachers are often difficult to locate, and in many cases may drop out of the work. It is questionable whether the employment of married women in the schools is advisable: on the one hand, it seems at present the only method to secure the necessary female teachers; on the other hand, the British Government is facing even at home the complications which the element of married women's work introduces into the labour market. True, Indian life is different, for the babies come with their mothers to school, and a kind Government supplies the necessary cradles and ayah, but there are undoubted hardships. "The life of the village schoolmistress has not many compensations; in addition to the long hours at school she has arduous home duties to perform. In many cases she is the sole breadwinner for five or six, none of whom consider it incumbent on them to help her with the household work. Rising at five in the morning or earlier, she has to begin her daily timetable, which extends over seventeen hours. It is marvellous that she is able to work as cheerfully as she does."[15] The permanent hope is in the widow, and it is encouraging to see a better proportion of them here. The spinster is at best available in mission schools for a short period till her marriage. Many trained Christian girls teach for several years, often living under the superintendence of the missionary, and make most efficient teachers. The supply of such, however, is in no way equal to the demand. It is difficult for one not fully acquainted with the Indian standard of life to judge of the financial aspect, but the impression gathered from the Government Reports is that increased salaries might

[15] *Public Instruction Report, Bombay*, p. 29.

attract a better class. There is a proverb that when begging fails it is well to learn to be a teacher. The salaries paid by mission agencies are, as a rule, slightly less than those paid by municipal authorities, just as the salaries of educational missionaries are less than the corresponding salaries at home. As regards training, a great effort is being made on all sides to secure that all the teachers either take a preliminary course or go up for the qualifying examination: at present the proportion is 44%. Any girl in a municipal school who shows any ability or desire can pass free of charge as a "stipendiary" to the Government Training Colleges with the stipulation that she shall teach thereafter with a salary for at least two years. Five mission schools have Normal divisions attached in which much the same conditions prevail. The city of Bombay has, however, no proper provision of opportunity. None of the Government Training Colleges are situated there, and, apart from Mr Chichgar's work, which is limited to the Parsi School Association, there is only a Saturday morning training class under the auspices of a United Missionary Committee, which is not largely attended. Poona, on the other hand, has two if not three Training institutions, and the circumstances seem to point towards redistribution. A Hindu girl is much more likely to continue her education if it does not entail leaving her relatives. Miss Wilson, Head mistress of the Girgaum High School, in a paper recently read at the Bombay Missionary Conference, emphasized the need of more funds to aid existing institutions, and of fixing a definite rate of salaries and a date after which none but trained teachers would be allowed in any school receiving a Government grant. The latter suggestion is possibly somewhat premature, as it might mean the closing of many schools or letting them lapse into the worse state of "unrecognized" institutions. The training of the Secondary teacher is a different problem. The impression current in Great Britain a decade ago that only people who knew nothing, or who could not teach, went to training colleges, seems still to prevail; moreover, there is no college where women teachers can receive a thorough Secondary training. The Inspectress' reply to an official inquiry as to the possibility of raising the general standard indicates the need of a central Government Training College with a graded system in the aided schools, and special salary grants to all Secondary schools staffed by trained teachers.[16] There does not, however, seem any prospect of direct action, either on the part of Government or of missionary societies. There are few vacancies in the Government Normal College, and though one woman, a Goanese student, has recently been studying there, the course is not adapted to women students. A few of the teachers go up for the Secondary Examination without a qualifying course or after attendance at a series of lectures given at the convent in Bombay. There is also a great lack of enthusiasm for the profession

[16] *Public Instruction Report, Bombay*, p. 16.

as such; teaching is felt to bemore or less a trade finishing at certain definite hours and limited in its influence to these. A most attractive set of lectures on various educational problems arranged by the Principal of the Government Normal College, had an average attendance of some seven out of possible hundreds. In the case of the women this is perhaps largely due to the enervating influence of the climate and the consequent lassitude after a long day's work, but there is undoubtedly a lack of some unifying and inspiring influence which would have a strong reflex effect on the tone of the schools.

The variation of the curriculum has to a certain extent been solved in this Presidency as regards the Primary stage. Bombay was the first province to issue a different set of readers for girls, and those now in use, comprising the study of heroes and heroines from a moral point of view, simple natural phenomena, domestic economy, etc., seem admirably adapted to them. The Code prescribes the usual elements with a study of forms, colours, familiar objects, drill, games, native accounts, and geography beginning in the third form, and Indian history in the fourth. The difficulty begins after the fourth Vernacular stage, corresponding to the first Anglo-Vernacular. After that stage the shadow of the Matriculation begins to fall, and so heavily that in the departmental schedule of studies, the highest Standard (VII. A.-V.) is left blank. Formerly this august portal could be passed very quickly by a well-crammed child. I met one

Parsi girl who entered the University at the age of thirteen. The age was raised by the Universities Commission to sixteen. A great controversy has recently raged round the place of the vernaculars in the University, and the question of the use of English as a medium of instruction in the school. In regard to the latter, the real educators argued the impossibility of the proper comprehension of a difficult subject through a foreign medium, and the tendency to parrot-like repetition of formula or fact, while the actively "Indian" party, failing to see the real point at issue, held that any other method would weaken the standard of English and handicap the Indian in public service. The Department have sanctioned the use of the vernacular till a later stage, but though some teachers spoke warmly in favour of this method, it has not yet gone beyond experiment. Certainly the teaching of history throughout the Matriculation forms seems exceedingly weak. The Code for the Anglo-Vernacular Standards in relation to the Matriculation, and the possible substitution for it of the School Final Examination, a more practical test, is, however, under Government consideration and the defects of the present Code need not be enlarged upon. The variation of the Code for girls is a further question, and the planning of a suitable curriculum is a matter which eminently lends itself to private enterprize. The de-orientalizing influence with Parsi girls is not so dangerous as with other Indian girls, but there is surely something wrong when " once a certificate, no more books " is a not infrequent cry. Some schools already vary their curriculum for girls: one mission report speaks of an alternative course better calculated to fit the girls for home life, leaving advanced mathematics, etc., to such only as have the necessary mental ability and physical strength. This effort has met with the approval of the Inspectress and of the more thoughtful parents. Matriculation has, however, in certain circles a distinct matrimonial value, and it is pathetic to see older girls, struggling at a distance of two forms from the desired goal, who would bitterly resent a change to a curriculum more suited to their diverse but not inferior powers.

It is here that the opportunity lies for English educators who can help Indian women through an exceedingly difficult transitional period to realize the meaning of modern culture, which, while possessing universal elements, must be evolved by every nation on the lines of its own genius and characteristics. In Bombay and in Poona there are Indian women who think deeply on these things, and who await as yet some constructive policy in the success of which, though the energy and initiative must be of the West, their share would not be lacking. If this constructive policy is to start from the Christian standpoint, if the Spirit of Christ is to dominate the new culture, the women of Anglo-Saxon countries must let their religion dominate them as never before, and win them out to the larger service.

IX

UNIVERSITY EDUCATION

"Travellers all in the land of the living,
In quest of the self it is best to be;
Comrades all in the getting and giving,
Prythee, tell us, what else are we?

Girls who go hopefully forth to the morrow,
In quest of the Women they wish to be,
Friends who look down on the fair, flying present,
Wistfully, lovingly—this are we."

From the "*Lal Bagh*" *Chronicle*.

A FIRM and steady step on the lower rungs of the ladder is a fair promise of the ultimate ascent, and after a time incredibly short since the first beginnings of Western education for women in India, the girl graduate is found issuing from the portals of the University.

Pioneer in many senses, with a world of idealistic possibilities surrounding her career, the Indian woman has proved the quality of her mental capacity; she has successfully stood the most strenuous of tests, and is prepared to take her part as a leader of her sex and as a contributor to the Feminist Movement. The member of Congress sees in her a political factor; the papers which advocate social reform hail her as a new force which will influence circles far beyond the reach of their propaganda ; the educator trusts that here at last is someone with the brain power and insight to indicate the true lines for the education of Indian women ; the missionary ponders on her possibilities for the Indian Church and the Indian home—while India, the real India, the silent multitude of India's women, knows little and cares less. This strange phenomenon seems no longer of their number ; she has stepped away with her new and dazzling robes from the old tradition, from the memories of the twilight and its tales to a new and untried world. And yet in a true sense she is still one with them, one with them in instinct, in thought, in hereditary traits, and fitted, as no Western could ever be, to act as the mediator betwixt the old and the new. The possibilities of the Indian woman graduate have to a certain extent been proved in subsequent careers ; on the other hand, the results of the whole system, as regards the average student, have not entirely justified the hopes built upon it. A brief examination of the actual facts and conditions will prove the best introduction to the problems which underlie them.

The five Universities of India—Calcutta, Madras, Bombay, Allahabad, and Lahore—the constitutions of which resemble that of the University of London, are open to any woman who can pass the qualifying entrance examination. Their subsequent studies must be conducted in a college duly recognized by Government and in affiliation with a University. These colleges vary as first and second grade according to the stage, Intermediate or Final B.A., to which they are able to take their students. Of the 175 colleges scattered over India 10 are specially women's colleges, but women are also found studying in mixed colleges under mission boards or Government. Of Government institutions it may practically be said that no sex barrier exists, except where a separate provision is made, as in the case of the Bethune College, Calcutta, and the same is true to a less extent of the mission institutions. Thus women students are found in the Elphinstone College, Bombay, in the Presidency College, Madras, and in the Government College, Rangoon, studying side by side with men under the same conditions. The Wilson College, Bombay, is an important example of the mixed mission college. The ten women's colleges in affiliation with one or other University [1] are as follows :—

	Number of Students.[2]
The Bethune College, Calcutta (first grade) .	40
The Diocesan College, Calcutta (first grade) .	32
The Isabella Thoburn College, Lucknow (first grade) (A.M.M.)	20
The Sarah Tucker College, Palamcottah (second grade) (C.M.S.) . . .	6
The Maharani's College, Mysore . .	

[1] There are in addition three Training Colleges.

[2] Approximate number only.

	Number of Students.
The Maharajah's College, Trevandrum .	
St Bede's Convent College, Simla (first grade)	
Auckland House School, Simla (second grade)	
European Girls' High School, Allahabad (second grade)	
Woodstock Girls' School, Landour (second grade)	

Of these, the last four are mainly for Eurasian girls, and fall outside the scope of our inquiry. With the exception of the Bethune and the two institutions in Native States, they are all under Christian management. The word "college" is highly misleading. The English reader pictures an institution parallel to Girton or Somerville, with a full staff of women tutors, supplemented by University lectures, whereas these colleges consist in most cases of small groups of girls, sometimes only one or two, who remain after Matriculation in their old school, studying for the most part under the same mistresses, and with little or no sense of any transition in their career. If no girls are fitted to proceed to the higher stages, the college as such may lapse for the time being; thus only students in training as teachers are returned in the Panjāb report for 1910, in spite of the two "colleges at Simla," whereas the Diocesan School appears officially for the first time in the Bengal report as a college with a most creditable number of students and an efficient staff. The one outstanding exception is the Isabella Thoburn College, where the college department is rigidly separated from the school, and where the collegiate atmosphere and sense of corporate life are dominant. A similar arrangement is being made in the new buildings of the Bethune College. Even in these two cases there is the linked High School under the same Principal, sharing in the interest of the staff. A women's college in the English sense of the word does not exist.

Passing to the students, the differences of creed, as indicated in the Quinquennial Returns of 1907, are seen in the annexed table. (See page 197.)

This proportion is on the whole maintained to-day, with the addition of a few Buddhist girls studying in Rangoon, and an increased proportion of Parsis in Bombay. The actual numbers show a remarkably small fluctuation within the last decade, and have not justified the hopes of those who expected a continuation of the fourfold increase of the preceding decade. In 1891 there were 45, in 1901, 177 Arts students. Taking some figures from local returns, we find the following :—[3]

Arts Students.	1901.	1906.	1910.
Bengal	55	24	47
United Provinces . .	49	38	45
Burma	8	2	12
Bombay . . .	30	57	76
Madras	?	?	37

Cf. also *Statistical Abstract, British India,* Table 105.

CLASSIFICATION OF COLLEGE STUDENTS BY RACE OR CREED

	Eurasian.	Native Christians.	Hindu.	Moham-medan.	Parsis.	Others.	Total.
Arts Colleges .	48	43	31	1	33	4	160
Medicine . .	40	19	4	...	11	2	76
Teaching . .	34	2	...	...	...	...	36
Law . . .	...	...	...	...	1	...	1
Medical School .	30	110	15	12	1	...	168
	152	174	50	13	46	6	441

A marked increase is shown only in the Bombay Presidency due to the influence of the Parsis. The students are drawn from varying ranks of society. Of the Hindu students about a quarter are Brahmans. Some are drawn from the new professional classes, who highly value education for their women, and can afford to pay for it; others from the poorer members of the Brāhma Samāj, who see in college education a prospect of a career for their daughters more in accordance with their enlightened ideas. Of the system of stipends it is difficult to form a judgment. Whereas in Britain a scholarship indicates special ability tested by competition, in India a Government or private stipend is in most cases available, at any rate in Bengal, for any girl who can pass the required average test. With luck she may possibly also secure another stipend to cover her board. The "average" girl is therefore apt to predominate far more largely than in the early stages of college education in Britain or America. There is also a lack of the element of hereditary culture, which has a very definite contribution to make in Indian life, and which may be the inheritance of the daughter as well as of the son. But where it is impossible to secure a genuinely competitive system and the only alternative is the closing of the college career to the really brilliant girl of the poorer classes, the question is a difficult one. In Calcutta, practically all the Bethune students belong to the Brāhma Samāj; in Bombay, where the line of separation between the Prārthanā Samāj and orthodoxy is very indefinite, and *parda* almost non-existent, orthodox Hindu students are to be found. It must be remembered, however, that these are essentially pioneers, and that the custom of early marriage or secluded widowhood still practically prevents any marked Hindu element amongst women students. In 1903 two Brahman ladies passed the Madras B.A. from the Maharani's College, Mysore, being the first of their caste there to do this.

The Parsi woman student needs no comment. Independent, bright, and alert, she holds her own in the mixed colleges of Bombay with the utmost equanimity, and has an unparalleled zest for examinations. In 1886, the first women students entered Wilson College, Ratanbai Ardeshir Vakil and her sister Meherbai, daughters of a leading Parsi solicitor. Several years before, the University had given women the right to go up for examination, but only one had made use of the permission. Ratanbai specialized in French, and was elected a Fellow in 1890. From then, till her early death in 1895, she taught French in the college, and warm testimony to her influence in the college and at home is borne by the Principal. "One could see how the education and culture of women, instead of creating a cleft in the life of the family, as is so often erroneously imagined by those who oppose the cause of female education in India, proves a means of strengthening its unity and elevating its whole character."[4] Her sister, Meherbai Vakil, is a much-respected medical woman in Bombay, and is typical of a growing number of Parsi students who have entered professional life with great credit. The brilliant career of Miss Cornelia Sorabji, a Christian Parsi, who holds the post of Legal Adviser to the Bengal Government for women in *parda*, is too well known to need emphasis. Two of her sisters are Head-mistresses of important Indian schools.

The Indian Christian woman student figures largely in the returns, and the pioneers of the movement were drawn from their ranks. This is the natural result of the educational policy pursued by the various missionary societies, and of the later age of marriage among Christians. Some of them are mentally very well fitted for their studies; there are others again who are largely subsidized by public or private funds, and possess ability to pass the average standard, but not sufficient mental power to gain full benefit from their training. Here, for instance, are two girls, daughters of an Indian clergyman, both passing well, and taking employment, one as a Mistress in a Government school, the other as an Inspectress in the Provincial Service; contrast with them a trembling, shrinking girl from a Native State who has received a scholarship from her State because she has matriculated and because she is one of an impoverished family of twelve, a par-

[4] Dr Mackichan, in Preface to Ratanbai's Translation of *Les Parsis*.

ticularly urgent case! Throughout her career the fear of failure and poverty intensifies the strain already possibly too great for a delicate constitution, and a girl who might have made an excellent Primary teacher is sacrificed on the altar of so-called higher education. And yet, as has already been indicated, the system affords the needed opportunity for the clever girl, and possesses this justification. The Christian students are mostly to be found in the Isabella Thoburn College, in Madras, and a few in Calcutta, chiefly at the Diocesan School and College. Since the latter was founded, about fifteen years ago, five B.A.'s have passed out and several F.A.'s.[5] New college buildings have recently been added with boarding accommodation for forty-five resident students. It is managed by the Community of St John Baptist, known generally as the Clewer Sisterhood. Miss Chunder Mukki Bose, M.A.,[6] to whose guidance the Bethune College has owed much of its prestige, and the late Lilavati Singh, M.A., Vice-Principal of the Isabella Thoburn College, stand out as the most prominent Indian Christian graduates, while the dramatic episode of Mrs Nvimabala Shome's graduation as B.A. at the same time as her husband in Calcutta, gave an object-lesson in

[5] F.A. — title given to those who have passed the First Arts examination, corresponding to "Intermediate." It is abolished by some of the Universities. *Cf.* p. 116.

[6] Now married to Pandit Keshavan.

matrimonial equality. She subsequently took her M.A. in England, and devoted much of her life to the organization of one of the mission High schools in Calcutta. Indian Christian graduates are to be found all over India undertaking responsible work with great credit.

The Mohammedan girl graduates cannot be discussed as a class, for even if we go back to the "glory of women," the Sheikha Shuhda of the Middle Ages, who lectured at Bagdad on literature and rhetoric, they are only found here and there as isolated figures. One Mohammedan girl of a well-known Bombay family passed first among girl candidates in the Bombay Presidency in 1910, and is now studying at Wilson College.

It will thus be seen that the women students of India are a very heterogeneous body, representing almost every shade of religious opinion, and varying possibly in their mental capacity to a greater extent than the women of other lands.

The question of the curriculum and of the nature of the studies required for the degree examinations has a very definite relation to the numerical problem stated above. Are these of a nature to attract increasing numbers? Are they sufficiently in accord with the Indian ideal of womanhood or with the aspirations of the reformers? The facts are worth analysis. From the first, the courses for men and women have been identical; no temporary expedient of a women's examination such as the Cambridge Higher Local, and the St Andrews L.L.A., has been adopted by any of the Indian Universities; women must cover the same ground as men or none at all. The various courses in Bombay are indicated in the accompanying diagram. The range of subjects is somewhat similar to that of the University of London; for the B.A. examination, the average candidate presents himself in English, Philosophy, or History, and one Classical or Modern language. There is a corresponding scientific course, English remaining compulsory throughout. The Intermediate examination covers a wider range of subjects. The details differ in different Universities, but the standard on the whole is similar. Calcutta alone requires a compulsory essay in the vernacular for the B.A., and the emphasis laid on Sanskrit and Arabic is not the same as that laid on Latin and Greek in the Western Universities. The Panjāb University has a separate Oriental Course, for which as yet no woman has entered. The M.A. is given on the results of further examination, and, in some Universities, after a fresh course of study. The proportion of students who go through the whole course is small: for every seventeen who pass the Intermediate, only five become Bachelors of Arts, and only one a Master.[7] I have been unable to procure separate figures for women, but apparently the proportion is even less, and there are very few women who have obtained the degree of M.A. The examination system of the Universities has been subjected to severe criticism, both

[7] *Administrative Problems of British India.* J. Chailley.

UNIVERSITY OF BOMBAY

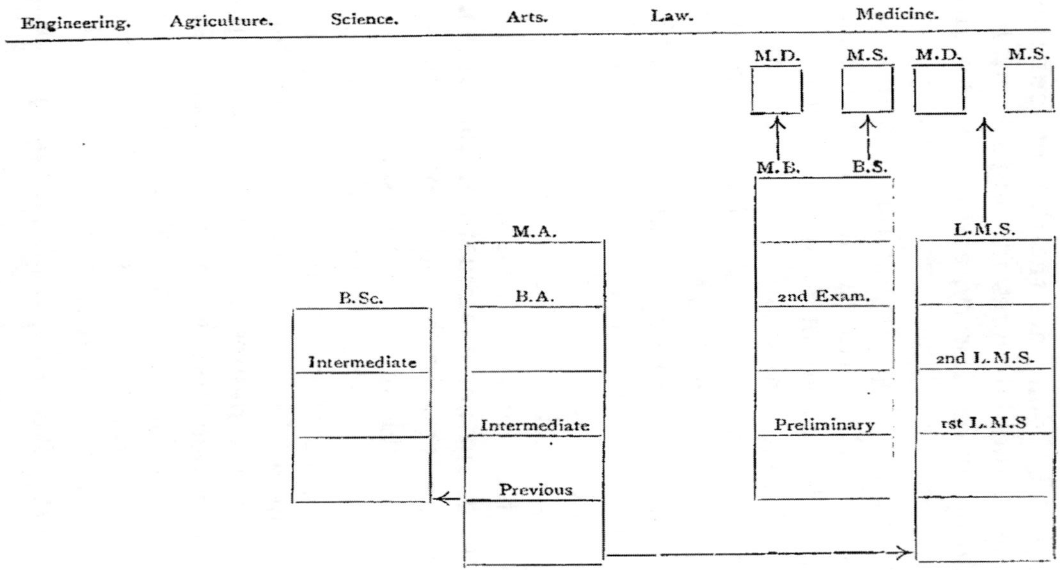

Matriculation (age 16).

NOTES.—The course in the other universities is somewhat similar.
Calcutta offers a degree as Bachelor of Teaching.
The degree of L.M. and S. is abolished in Calcutta and the Panjāb, but retained in the meantime in Bombay and in Madras after a six years' course.
Matriculation age in Madras and the Panjāb is fifteen.

Quinquennial Review of Progress of Education in India, vol. ii. p. 65.

by enlightened Indians and by Europeans, the chief indictments being embodied in Lord Curzon's Universities' Commission Report of 1904, and we find tentative reforms in the subsequent Act. The "yattering" graduate who knows nothing and can decide nothing, but who can repeat yard after yard from any prescribed text-book, is the byword of those who wish to taunt India, and there is a germ of truth in the reproach. The effort to impart the highest Western culture through Indian teachers who have only partially assimilated it themselves, must prove to some extent unsatisfactory. Since the Public Service Commission in 1886, Indians have been admitted to the Educational Service in much larger numbers: for example, the Presidency College in Calcutta had in 1880 a complete staff of English professors and Oriental specialists; in 1911, only eight are English and twenty-three Indian, though in the meantime the number of pupils has increased from 350 to 700.[8] It is possible that here real efficiency has been sacrificed from the commendable motives of economy and a desire to utilize the Indians in their own Universities. To command a supply of the best men from home would involve a heavy financial strain, and yet, unless the Oriental, who can live on a smaller salary, has spent some years in Europe, he is hardly fitted to guide a University where the curriculum largely consists of Western subjects. It is interesting to find Mr Gokhale emphasizing

[8] *Indian Unrest.* V. Chirol.

the need of studying in a foreign University as a preliminary to professional work in India.[9] It is the presence of a fully equipped English staff (who are there for other reasons than the mere acquisition of a " living " wage) which forms the attractive force of a Mission college to the ambitious young Indian. The whole question is an exceedingly difficult one, and has been fully discussed recently by both Mr Chailley and Sir Valentine Chirol ; it is raised here only in so far as it affects the women who study in mixed colleges. It should also be noted that there is no English lady on the staff of Bethune College, the only Government college for women. The feminine counterpart of the typical graduate indicated above is apparently his decided superior, for the Indian feminine virtues of modesty and reticence come to her aid, and she does not air her acquired knowledge. Still her knowledge is only acquired, not yet assimilated, and there is a lamentable lack of books in her study. The library at Bethune College is not utilized to the same extent as one in a corresponding English institution. Actual personal contact with some of the Indian students is a pathetic experience, as we are forced to realise how little real grit there is behind their text-book knowledge. They have gained no broad outlook on life : a tired brain has struggled through so many hours a day of lecture work and book work, and no energy is left for thought ! Climatic and constitutional conditions

[9] *Administrative Problems.* J. Chailley.

account, to a certain extent, for this result ; lack of hereditary culture to a still greater degree ; but it is fostered largely by the conditions under which the girls have studied, and by the failure of Anglo-Saxon women to give them of their best. Where the women study apart in the additional classes of their former High schools they certainly receive individual attention, which results in creditable passes, and this is possibly the chief merit of a system which has little to be said for it from other points of view. The complete staff of the Isabella Thoburn College, the well-utilized library, and the reputation which its graduates have won throughout India, are facts which should be noted in this connexion. The Diocesan College is establishing a similar tradition.

There is another side to University life than the purely intellectual, namely, the human and personal. This, with all its varied manifestations in the common pursuit of sport or of music, in the discussion of social problems and of mental difficulties, or still more in the gentle art of doing nothing, lends the charm to college days and is perhaps the more dominant factor in after life. The influence of certain personalities, men or women, who can be trusted, who can look at life's problems from the same point of view as their students, and are able to throw light on their difficulties with the ripeness of experience and to lead them to a new moral or religious outlook, is often in the long run more powerful than that of the actual literature studied. If the University or college fails as a school of character it has failed of its *raison d'être*. Precisely on this ground has the strongest indictment recently been made against the Indian system. "There has been no more deplorable feature in the recent political agitation than the active part taken in it by Indian schoolboys and students."[10] A University course inevitably shakes the foundations of their thought, and in many cases has resulted in a revolt from all former moral or religious standards of conduct without providing a new basis for life. Under a stricter *régime*, with liberal grants and every possible encouragement of private hostels where religious instruction is possible, an effort is being made to combat this lack in the training of character. The case of women students presents certain parallel features, and also difficulties peculiarly its own.

The larger proportion of women students in Bombay in attendance at the mixed classes are living in their own homes; a few from the country are in residence at the Students' Hostel of the Missionary Settlement for University Women,[11] where, though the majority are Christian, students of other faiths can be received under special arrangements. A Jain lady was at one time in residence there. This hostel is in close proximity to both the Wilson and the Grant Medical Colleges, and supplies a real need, but its residents so far have not been

[10] *Indian Unrest.* Chirol.

[11] *Cf.* Report from Secr. M.S.U.W., 74 Denison House, Vauxhall Bridge Road, London.

Missionary Settlement for University Women
Students' Hostel, Bombay

very numerous. The women students of Bombay as a whole have no corporate life of their own; they may attend some of the joint debating societies and kindred meetings, but do not as a rule take part. Their common rooms offer rather a geographical *pied-à-terre* than a means of social unity. As regards athletics, badminton is pursued in a somewhat spasmodic way in one college, and by invitation to the Principal's house in another, but the question of exercise in relation to non-resident students is always a moot point in a tropical climate. Some attempt to develop social life is made by the women graduates from British or Colonial Universities who are in charge of the students' hostel; they visit the common rooms of two of the colleges, and occasionally organize debates or kindred functions at the hostel, to which the residents may invite other students. The writer was present at one such debate on the question of educating men and women on similar lines, and the opinions expressed by some of the Indian girls are embodied in much of the foregoing. This influence is also of a religious nature, being in connexion with the Students' Branch of the Young Women's Christian Association, and indirectly counts for much. It is, however, an extraneous one, and therefore many of the students, especially in the Government colleges, are beyond its reach. With their actual lecturers they can have, in the nature of the case, little or no personal contact, and the real need seems to be the introduction of women on the staff of these colleges, together with the tutorial system, which has proved itself so useful in mixed non-residential universities in Britain. The case is very strongly put by Mr Covernton, who was till recently Principal of the Elphinstone College.

"It is becoming a problem how to provide accommodation and adequate supervision for these girls. It is ridiculous to expect that young unmarried graduates, fresh from Oxford and Cambridge, can mould the minds and characters of Parsi, much less of Brahman girls; while the training of Eurasian girls is still more difficult. Moreover, the close association of male and female involved in a mixed education is so totally opposed to the traditions of the East, as well as so fraught with possibilities of evil, that in my opinion the system is rather a barrier than an encouragement to female education.—A special lecturer and tutor of female students should be appointed to the Elphinstone College. She should be a British graduate, and a member of the Indian Educational Service. Her subject should preferably be English, because it is very easy to get women well qualified to teach that subject. She would take complete charge of the girls' studies in that subject, and would in addition supervise their general reading, their games, and most important of all their manners and conduct."[12] As regards conduct the general bearing and influence of these girls in the mixed colleges has been most creditable in very trying circumstances, but there is

[12] *Public Instruction Report, Bombay*, 1910.

certainly a need to relax the evident tension of the position, which is little in accordance with Oriental ideas.

The condition of the women students in Madras who attend the mixed colleges is somewhat similar. There is an excellent hostel managed by the Students' Branch of the Young Women's Christian Association, where students of all faiths can reside, and former pupils of the mission schools can still remain in connexion with them. I understand that the same strain exists here, with the consequent lack of energy for any corporate life. An English woman graduate writes from Madras of the great need in South India of a first-grade women's college.

In Calcutta conditions are entirely different; there is a good hostel in connexion with the Bethune College, and the Christian girls who attend it are resident in their former schools. There are only a few non-residential students, but as the colleges attended by the Arts students are very small, the system assimilates to the tutorial, and there is ample opportunity for contact between student and lecturer. In the Bethune College, however, where the majority of teachers are men, the conflict with Oriental ideas arises again, and one is not surprised, apart from other reasons, at the absence of Moslem or orthodox Hindu girls. Here again it seems unfortunate that there is no corporate life or unity amongst the women students as a whole, or even in the Bethune hostel itself. In the latter it would depend entirely on Indian initiative, and though one would expect it to assume a different form from the customary Saxon one, its entire absence can only be accounted for by unfavourable conditions.

The corporate life of the Isabella Thoburn College has already been emphasized; a glance at the students' *Lal Bagh Chronicle* is enough to convince the reader of its reality, and of its characteristically Indian nature.

The case of the Indian woman medical student must be considered apart from the life of the Arts colleges. As a rule few women, except an occasional Parsi, pass from the one to the other, and there is little contact. It is unnecessary here to emphasize the need for every possible encouragement for Indian women to take up the practice of medicine. The sorrows and sufferings of Indian women behind the *parda*, who would rather face death than admit a male practitioner, are well known. If to some the statements made by missionary writers seem exaggerated, they have only to turn to the petition presented to the Viceroy in 1890 by the medical women practising in India to find evidence of the saddest facts. Indian medical students are divided broadly into two classes, those who study in one of the four Government colleges affiliated to one or other of the chief Universities, and those who study in the medical schools for a very much lower qualification.[13]

[13] There are at present in hospital work in India 47 women medicals of the first grade (including Englishwomen), 92 assistant surgeons, and 67 hospital assistants, practitioners, etc. *Cf. Report of the Countess of Dufferin's Fund*, 1911.

Of the first class again some are genuine University students going up for the degrees indicated on page 204, while others are content merely with the college diploma which qualifies for practice in India. The medical schools, of which there are twenty-seven in different parts of India, are "intended primarily for the instruction of candidates for employment in Government Service as hospital assistants, but many of their pupils also go into private practice." [14] They confer the title of sub-assistant-surgeon. A few women students are to be found in the former class: in 1907 it included thirty-four Indian women in all, and there has not been any marked increase in recent years. An even smaller number of these take the highest qualification. All that has been said of the strained life of the women Arts students applies even more strongly to the medicals. It is a very hard and difficult life, and there is little in the environment to lessen the burden. The statistics of the medical schools on the other hand show a larger figure, 138 in 1907, with a considerable increase in recent years. It is in these schools that the administrators of the Countess of Dufferin's Fund,[15] which has done so much for the medical treatment of women, place most students, though some are also to be found studying in the Universities. Three of these

[14] *Quinquennial Report*, vol. i.

[15] Founded in 1884, the total value of hospital buildings connected with the Fund is now 50 lakhs. 90 students are in receipt of stipends. *Cf.* Report.

schools are specially women's schools—the North India Medical School for Christian Women at Ludhiana, the female branch of the Agra Medical School, and one centre in the Bombay Presidency with some half-dozen pupils. The work of the former, as it illustrates by contrast the serious problem of the mixed medical schools and colleges, is worthy of special notice. This school, which is under the management of a private committee, including members of the Indian Medical Service, was originally founded in 1894 through the agency of seven missionary societies working in the United Provinces and the Panjāb. Its aim was to secure "that the young Christian women who pass through a medical course, and then go out to Government or Native State or Mission Hospital work, should be so safeguarded and trained that they shall be worthy representatives of the religion they profess."[16] The dangers of the joint-system of instruction in all subjects, with unlimited association in hospitals and museums, is apparent in every centre, with its consequent effect in some cases of bringing "female education and emancipation into discredit." A letter of application to the Ludhiana School throws some light on prevalent conditions :—

"I require a Female Hospital Assistant for my Hospital, and am very anxious to get one who has been trained under Medical Women. As your

[16] *A Problem and its Solution*, E. M. Brown, M.A., M.D. (Procurable from 36 Fairfield Road, Bromley, Kent.)

School is the only one in India of this sort, would you be kind enough to let me have one? This is not a Mission Hospital but one for *parda* Moslem women only, under the Dufferin Fund, and it is essential that the Assistant be respectable. (This I find rather difficult to get amongst the class trained under males.) It is perhaps against your rules to supply Dufferin Fund Hospitals, but I hope you will stretch a point and oblige me by letting me have one, as I have had a great deal of trouble for the past year with Assistants."

The students of the Ludhiana School flock from all parts of India for the benefit of this tuition under qualified medical women. There are at present some twenty-seven Indian Christian students and five Eurasians, taking the four years' course, while some thirty others are training as "compounders." The linked women's hospital,[17] with a record of 1300 in-patients and 26,000 new out-patients in 1910, affords the necessary opportunity for practice. The staff is drawn from India, Britain, and America, and consists of eight fully qualified medical women. The record of the school is one of slow and steady progress in efficiency and numbers, and the latest stage is the proposed affiliation to the Panjāb University, the negotiations for which are progressing favourably. Under these conditions the school would be able as a college to send students up for the M.B., B.S.

[17] Further hospital practice might be available in Ludhiana.

examination, and the Government students would be transferred to it from Lahore. The hostel life of the students is under careful superintendence, and arrangements are being made for the accommodation of non-Christian students. The contrast between the life here and that of women medical students in Bombay or Calcutta is marked; and if it be argued that the highest professional ability cannot be obtained with so limited a hospital roll, there is surely need for modifying in some way the conditions at these centres. Two Government hostels for women medical students exist in Calcutta in close proximity to the two hospitals;[18] the question, however, concerns not only hostel life but professional training under circumstances which will not injure character. The complete separation in the London and Edinburgh Schools of Medicine for Women affords a striking contrast. A certain number of Indian students, perhaps one or two a term, come over for a full or supplementary course in British colleges, as this qualification secures a better post on return.

To sum up, the problem respecting Indian women students, in both Arts and Medicine, arises, apparently, from the need of a numerical increase, from the lack of conditions so adapted to Oriental ideas that the highest courses shall be open without difficulty to women of all ranks, and from the lack of a curriculum calculated to raise the standard of the intellectual work done. Moreover,

[18] The Y.W.C.A. has student branches in these hostels.

Ludhiana School of Medicine—Hospital Court Yard with Patients

mental training must be combined with such opportunities for the development of character as shall ensure to Indian women the leaders they require.

These needs interact, and affect one another; the numerical problem depends, as we have seen, on certain conditions of Indian society, and also on the attractive force of the education offered and its appeal to Indian ideas, as well as on the possibility of pursuing it under conditions which shall not be too utterly opposed to the tradition of the country. With the increase in the numbers receiving Secondary education there has not been a corresponding increase in the college courses. Mr Covernton, in the quotation given above, further emphasizes this, and points to the real need of Bombay, for which the appointment of a woman tutor would only be a temporary expedient. "If the conditions of University education were in accord with Oriental ideas of women's functions, the number would go up by leaps and bounds. I am confident that the time is ripe for the creation in Bombay of a women's college managed by a staff of Oxford or Cambridge women graduates."[19] The spontaneous movement amongst Indian gentlemen to organize high-class schools, where, if desired, *parda* can be kept, points to further possibilities. At present, if a Mohammedan or Hindu girl of high caste, who had been educated in some such school, or privately, desired to take a University course,

[19] *Bombay Public Instruction Report*, 1910.

there would be no opportunity for her doing so. A Mohammedan lady, whose daughter was being educated in one of the mission schools in Bombay, told the writer she could not think of letting her attend any college in that city, though she was anxious for her to have University education. The only possible course was an English college, such as Cheltenham. The migration to England of Indian women Arts' students has, so far, not been extensive; about a dozen have studied at Cambridge, Oxford, and Cheltenham; a larger number may have gone to America. The missionary societies which struck out a bold policy for attracting men by their great Christian colleges have not made any corresponding move to meet the new situation in women's education. The one or two women's colleges which exist are created so predominantly for Christian girls that they attract only isolated pupils of other faiths, and these not of the most influential classes.[20] It seems strange that in Great Britain the highest education for women should be to a certain extent apart, with the necessary contact carefully chaperoned, whereas in India, with a very different tradition of womanhood, one girl may sit alone in a class of over a hundred students. It may be argued that the best way to overcome this tradition is to ignore it, and that it should not be yielded to in any way, least of all in the case of Higher education, where the students have pre-

[20] Exceptions exist in the Diocesan College, Calcutta, in the case of non-residents.

sumably risen above it. Some English women of experience in India take this bold attitude. On the other hand it is of the highest importance in any transitional stage to secure leaders from every stratum of the population ; and if education be the only safe lever for the uplift of women in India, it seems a strategic mistake practically to close its highest stages to those whose families hold by a certain type of decorum which prohibits co-education.

By adaptation of the curriculum is not meant in any sense the lowering of the intellectual standard nor the introduction of the element of domestic economy and so called " feminine subjects " which are necessary at a lower stage, but rather a re-arrangement of studies which shall ensure more individual research and a fuller comprehension of the material studied. The revision of the curriculum is at present under consideration in at least one of the Universities, and is a matter for experts. The action of the University of Cambridge in permitting women candidates to go up for Honours courses only, and the success which has attended women candidates for the Triposes, suggest the advantage of specialized studies in the case of women. Mrs Satthianadhan's opinion of the effect of University education on women is illuminating. " It will make women more methodical, more orderly in their arrangements, more precise, and better able to weigh causes and results."[21] A three years' specialized course

[21] *Indian Ladies' Magazine.*

would tend in many ways to develop these qualities, and would possibly produce the new and more thorough type of teaching which is so greatly needed in the schools. The intellectual strain which is so marked a feature at present might in this way be lessened without detrimental effect upon real intellectual development.

Towards the end of last century, it seemed as if the goal of the women's educational movement in Great Britain might be reached by the formation of a Women's University with federal colleges. Various reasons have led rather to their taking a parallel place in the existing Universities, though still under somewhat anomalous conditions, so far as Oxford and Cambridge are concerned. The American solution is a different one. Vassar, Bryn Mawr, Wellesley, Mount Holyoake, and others have their separate degrees and completely separated life. It is possible that the solution of the Indian problem will rather follow these latter lines, and there are indications of this ideal, somewhat nebulously outlined, in the writings of leading Indian women. Such a Women's University with affiliated colleges in the different large centres might establish a new era and a new tradition in the education of women. A competent staff of Indian women-graduates, whose presence would secure the students from de-orientalizing influences, and of English women-graduates competent to teach on specialized lines, would raise the educational standard. The complete separation of such colleges from the

High schools would render a corporate life possible, and give to the Indian girl graduates the opportunity of carrying on their studies in congenial and stimulating surroundings. "To them, too, college life might bring that joyous springtime of youth, friendship, and unfettered delight of study and leisure which have hitherto been withheld from them."[22] The Maharani of Baroda notes in her recent book[23] the tendency of women's education in Europe to take a too exclusively literary form, and the consequent overcrowding of certain professions. While there is no danger that the teaching profession will be overcrowded in India for decades to come, the warning is not without its value. Such a University might have affiliated with it colleges of Indian Domestic Science and Economy, but the theory for this has yet to be worked out.

It may seem to some readers, especially to those rightly imbued with the Eastern principle of *festina lente,* that the day for women's colleges in India has not yet come, and that all available strength should be concentrated on Secondary education ; and yet, on the other hand, the crux of the whole educational problem may be found here. Miss Emily Davies, who by universal consent stands as the chief pioneer of the movement in Britain, realized from the first that the reform

[22] Alice Zimmern on the aims of the Girton pioneers in *Renaissance of Girls' Education.*

[23] *Position of Women in Indian Life,* by Her Highness the Maharani of Baroda.

in girls' education must begin at the top. The same principle is seen in the history of Cheltenham Ladies College (founded 1853), and the early efforts of Miss Beale to face the same problem of the need of teachers, which is felt in every Indian school to-day. " Her efforts show how hard it was to found a school before the reformation of the higher education had given the necessary stimulus from above. It was a case of making bricks without straw." [24] The proximity of certain dates is suggestive. In 1869, the " Girton Pioneers " first met at Hitchin to read for the examinations of the University of Cambridge. In 1872, the Girls' Public Day School Company was founded, and in 1879 the Oxford Women's Halls were opened. The two movements are of necessity contemporaneous, and cannot be viewed as successive stages towards the same end.

The beginning exists in India ; much excellent pioneer work has been done, and it now remains to raise the whole movement to a status from which its future development on Indian and womanly lines would be assured.

[24] *Renaissance of Girls' Education.* A. Zimmern.

X

THE RELIGIOUS ELEMENT IN EDUCATION

" Education, education—education about what? Education about matter, mere material things, thoughts and ideas. Education, according to the Vedas, is the opening of the petals of the mind-lotus to the rays of the spiritual sun, and that is what we now want first."

—Swami Baba Pramânand Bhârati.

THE analysis of the religious element in education is a deep and subtle problem, and yet, at the same time, this element is the touchstone by which all systems of education are ultimately tested. The formation of independent thought and judgment, and of an upright character, spontaneously moral, may lead in adolescent years to the attainment of some unifying philosophy of life which shall dominate and satisfy the religious nature. The successful quest of this during the " silent period," and the re-interpretation of it during a college career, must be the aim of all education. How is this aim to be achieved? The separation of religion from education in a Christian country, where morality is under the corporate sanction of inherited religious tradition, may be a dangerous experiment, but it is made under the supposition that the influence of home and Church will supplement the teaching at school. In India, a country of conflicting faiths, all in a period of transition, and withal a country of deep religious instinct, the case is different. There is no corporate sanction: religion and moral principles are not necessarily kindred terms; the influence of school and of home are often diverse, and thus the former, if it is in any sense to be the builder of character, must include religion as the only unifying educational factor. Theoretically, this statement is justified and endorsed, not only by missionary enthusiasts, but by official opinion and by Indian sentiment in so far as it is articulate; its practical endorsement, on the other hand, is one of the most difficult problems of Indian administration. A brief sketch of the attitude of Government in the past, and of the modern desire for its modification may serve to show the relation which this question bears to the present development of women's education.

The great educational Charter of 1854 established the Indian system on the only basis which seemed in accord with our whole Indian policy—that of religious neutrality; but it was not, as is sometimes erroneously supposed, an endorsement of a wholly secular policy. The Government could not of itself undertake direct religious teaching in its own schools, but the system of "grants-in-aid" with which it endowed the voluntary schools was "based on an entire abstinence from interference with the religious instruction conveyed in the schools assisted." "The framers of this Despatch entertained the hope that under its provisions Hindu, Mohammedan, and Christian managers would supply, each class in its own particular way, what was already known to be a great defect of the course of instruction in Government institutions. The same hope was one of the chief reasons that led the Education Commission to make and the Government of India to adopt the recommendation that 'the improvement and extension of institutions under private management be the principal care of the Department.'"[1] At the same time many of its members believed that even the more secular instruction given in the Government schools would remove ignorance and superstition, and ultimately pave the way towards the acceptance of Christianity. Moreover, definite provision was made for the inquiring mind. "The Bible is, we understand, placed in the libraries of the colleges and schools, and the pupils are freely able to consult it. This is as it should be; and, moreover, we have no desire to prevent, or discourage, any explanations which the pupils may of their own free-will ask from the masters on the subject of the Christian religion, provided that such information be given out of school hours." The agitation of those who wished a more definitely Christian attitude to be adopted aimed at voluntary teaching of the

[1] *Unrest and Education in India.* Wm. Miller, D.D., LL.D., C.I.E.

Bible, where a suitable teacher could be procured, and a suggestion of teaching the Indian religions parallel with it is scarcely found. The argument, as it might be presented to an Indian expostulating in favour of neutrality, is thus put in Sir John Lawrence's Despatches :—"We offer you the Bible in our Government schools because we believe it to be for your inestimable good if you choose to listen to it. We do not wish you to study it unless you do so voluntarily. But you cannot expect us to help in teaching your religion, which we do not believe to be true. That you can do for yourselves."[2] "The Indian religions ought not to be taught; they have ample means of their own for doing this." It should be noted that at this time the Samājes had not arisen, nor the Hindu reform movement, and that the Western comprehension of things Indian and religious was much more limited than it is now. The Despatch of 1859, after reviewing the various arguments for the modification of the "secular" policy, finally sums up—"They [Her Majesty's Government] are unable, therefore, to sanction any modification of the rule of strict religious neutrality, as it has hitherto been enforced in the Government schools, and it accordingly remains that the Holy Scriptures being kept in the library, and being open to all the pupils who may wish to study them, and the teachers being at liberty to afford instruction and explanations regarding

[2] Despatches on Christianity in India—Sir John Lawrence (*Times* Reprint).

them to all who may voluntarily seek it, the course of study in all Government Institutions be, as heretofore, confined to secular subjects."[3] The emphasis on the place of the aided school and the Government school has varied in the different periods of Indian administration and in different localities, but in the main in the education of boys the Government or municipal school has predominated. Its possible religious influence has been negative; and while there is no record of the English teacher expounding the Bible to inquiring minds after school hours, as the Despatches fondly picture, there is ample evidence that the Western education introduced sapped the foundations of ancient belief and substituted no new positive sanction of moral principles. The Hindu and Mohammedan effort of the early days on Western lines was also, with the exeption of Aligarh College, largely on a secular basis. Thus, the place of definite religious teaching was confined to the schools under missionary management, and though their influence, especially in South India, has been enormous, it can in no sense be considered conterminous with Western education in India. A predominantly secular education has therefore produced its own fruits, and a discussion of it when so much literature already exists on the subject is superfluous.

The modern reaction is manifest in popular speeches, in the Press, and in Government reports. An Indian writer pleads that the Durbar boon of

[3] Despatch of the Secretary of State, 1859.

additional grants for education is no boon, but a curse, if it perpetuate only the "nauseatingly materialistic, all-intellectual, and soul-killing system," and is not in consonance with the "natural ideals, national aspirations, and the world-old mental characteristics"[4] of the Indian people. It would be easy to multiply quotations in grandiloquent language, which, for all their quaintness, have a strong element of truth. Parallel with the plea for religious instruction, and to a certain extent confused with it, is the plea for moral instruction, either apart from or based on religion. The most trustworthy evidence as to the extent of this demand and its somewhat incoherent nature was given at the Government Educational Conference held recently in Allahabad, when a whole day was devoted to the subject of Moral and Religious Education. The preceding questionnaire inquired (*a*) how far moral lessons were included in the ordinary Primary readers, (*b*) whether special moral text-books were in use, (*c*) whether direct moral instruction was given and appreciated, (*d*) whether the trend of public opinion was really in favour of moral instruction in the schools, and finally (*e*) whether any divergent views thereon were based on differences of creed. Most of the provinces reported a certain element of moral instruction in the shape of stories and poetry in the readers, with the comment that these were

[4] "King George and the Hindoos," *XIX Century*, January 1912.

mainly used as reading or grammar lessons, or else were too didactically taught to have any lasting effect. Certain moral text-books are in use, but these are mainly of a religious nature and found in the newer Indian schools. The "Sanatana Dharma" series, issued by the Central Hindu College, Benares, which attempts to deal only with basal principles of religion, is used by the Surat municipality, in Mysore, in Baroda and elsewhere, but is not generally acceptable to orthodox Hindus. The classic Bhaghavat Gita—an eclectic synopsis reconciling different systems of Hindu philosophy and religion—is also taught as a class-book in the higher classes of certain schools in Bengal which were started as rivals to mission schools. The Anjuman-i-Islamia, Lahore, also prepares books for both Primary and Secondary classes in Mohammedan schools, and in these again moral instruction is imparted through religious references. Moral text-books pure and simple are not used except occasionally those of the International Moral League in some of the hostels in Baroda and elsewhere. As regards lessons in direct moral teaching, apart from religion, there seem to be exceedingly few. A few debating societies exist for this purpose. One school reports a weekly lecture thereon, but the boys of the school are credited with stoning a visiting cricket team which had defeated them! Moral instruction combined with religion is more common than it is thought in the Indian aided schools, and various instances are on record.

The old-fashioned Koranic schools and Sanskrit "*tols*" are steeped in religion. "To describe the system of moral training in such institutions would be to write an account of the rites and tenets of the Hindu and Mohammedan religions."[5] With two exceptions the reports show in detail a general state of dissatisfaction with things as they are, and a desire for definite moral instruction combined with a strong preference for a religious basis where such could be made possible. The words "moral instruction" seem also to have become a sort of shibboleth. "People are also rather vague as to what comes under the head of religion or morality." A Brahman student is instanced as having devoted much time to religion, which was found to mean "breathing exercises." "There are a few of exceptional intelligence who hold that the teaching of morality must be based on religion. These would advocate the teaching of a religion, or rather a combination of religious truths that all men could agree on." "The public mind in Bengal is not ripe for the idea of moral instruction totally severed from religion." At the same time it is noticed that little advantage has as yet been taken of the opportunity to teach religion in the Government schools in the United Provinces and in Burma. The restrictions which surround it in the former and the recent date of the permission for it in the latter may possibly account for this.

The bulk of the answers to the questionnaire

[5] *Allahabad Conference Report*, 1911.

issued by the Conference may be summed up in respect of moral instruction as follows: it is inefficient, unless impressed by the personality of the teacher, and unless based on religion; a merely moral system can be accepted only in circumstances which completely prohibit the religious element. Combined with the desire for it is a certain healthy scepticism as to whether moral instruction can be imparted in small doses, and whether the more effective influence is not the general discipline and tone of the school. The discussions at the Conference, which represented every shade of official and religious opinion, followed the same line. The emphatic testimony of Christian and Mohammedan dwelt on the need for the religious sanction, the Hindu testimony on the same need, but also on the impossibility for Hindus of finding a common ground amongst themselves. "No teaching which rests merely upon the basic principles of religion will be accepted by Hindus as taking the place of directly orthodox religion." [6] The incorporation of moral teaching in the Government system by means of a general text-book seemed at best only a makeshift, and did not meet with universal approval.

The evidence of the Allahabad Conference reveals a need and a deadlock. The country needs morality taught under religious sanction, but how can a Government pledged irrevocably to religious neutrality provide this? The granting of equal

[6] G. K. Gokhale.

opportunity in the Government and municipal schools for parallel instruction in the various faiths, as Sir Valentine Chirol suggests,[7] would not meet the special case of the Hindus, and might possibly complicate the position of the mission schools. The disintegration of a school where rival influences were at work would further render impossible the unity necessary to tone and discipline. The solution of the problem seems rather to lie in the *religious influence of a single kind,* and this is possible only in the aided schools. The development of these, and the allocation of a greater proportion of public funds to them, especially now that the indigenous Indian schools of the newer type are developing religious instruction, would be in historical continuity with the principles of 1854, and would not contradict the principles of neutrality.

The problem of female education was not considered separately at Allahabad, and there was no reference throughout the discussion to girls' schools. But though girls' education may be assumed to be some fifty years behind that of boys, a great deal of the report has a very direct bearing on our subject as indicating dangers to be avoided and a more profitable course to be pursued. The whole question is even more vital in their case, as the removal of religious and moral principles would be fraught with consequences even more serious to the community. How far is the education of women in India undermining

[7] *Indian Unrest.* Sir Valentine Chirol.

their religious beliefs? How far is this influence being counteracted by moral teaching, or by definite instruction in the principles of their own religion or of Christianity?

As regards the vast proportion of girls who attain a mere literacy in the Primary schools, the disintegrating influence can scarcely be said to have begun; on the other hand, in the Government and municipal schools there is a lack of constructive influence guiding them towards that which is true, honest, and of good report. Exceptional women amongst the few trained teachers may use the opportunity afforded by the moral lessons in the readers, but only the exceptional women. Schools started for girls by Indian societies have arisen mostly in the later period of religious revival, and some of their Primary schools are saturated with religion. In so far as an outsider can judge, this tends mainly to the abnormal development of the repetitive faculty. In the Christian Primary schools the influence of the Biblical instruction given naturally varies enormously according to the method of the Indian teacher and according to the frequency of the visits of the English missionary. The writer has watched a Scripture lesson given by an Indian teacher to a group of Bengali girls aged about eight years; their attention, response, and independent questions compared favourably with those of English children of the same age. It is also part of the ordinary experience of the zenana visitor to find the influence and memory of these school lessons still alive amongst those who have long left school.

In the Secondary and Training stages, the question is totally different, and the beginning of the influence which has proved so disastrous on the men's side is already felt. The Head of one Government Normal school stated, "Our education cannot fail to undermine their previous ideas," and then commented afterwards on the ineffectiveness of the moral instruction she was trying to introduce. In some of the Government schools where the Principal is a woman of special ability and tact, moral instruction is given, but as a rule it is not attempted. In the Government mixed colleges there is naturally no influence of this nature. In the Indian schools religious instruction is the rule, its character, as indicated in the reports to the Allahabad Conference, differing enormously in different places. In some it is carefully thought-out moral instruction, linked with those ideas in the particular religious faith which bear it out. The Benares school is a typical example of this; the whole school join in morning *puja* to Sarasvati, the goddess of learning, and there are special times during the week for instruction from the Sanatana Dharma series. The new Hindu High school in Bombay is visited once a week for the purpose by a Brahman, and a small catechism of a more orthodox nature is in use. The only Buddhist girls' Anglo-Vernacular school in Burma is marked by a strong religious tone. Instruction is given daily by an elderly priest to the whole school together, " in order that they may feel religion is the most important thing in daily life and therefore must be daily." A specimen of the catechism used is typical :—

" What are the three things to seek daily ?
  Truth, Knowledge, Righteousness.
" What will you do when you go home ?
  We will do salutation to our parents.
" And afterwards ?
  We will do our work.
" And in the morning ?
  Our first thought will be of righteousness."[8]

Religious and moral instruction is now given in most of the Parsi schools of Bombay under the auspices of a special Zoroastrian Association. This is, I understand, an innovation of the last ten years. In the schools under committees of different faiths the same difficulty is felt as in the Government schools. It is solved in one case by carefully prepared moral intsruction on an eclectic basis, in another by parallel religious observances. There is no uniformity in practice, but the universal attempt is a clear proof that the Indian desire for education on a religious basis for their daughters is genuine.

The Christian factor so far has been the predominating one, for the " bulk of female Secondary education is provided by the missionaries."[9] The

[8] The quotation is from a verbal translation given during the visit to the school.

[9] *Quinquennial Report*, vol. i. p. 257.

religious atmosphere is one of unity and simplicity. It is part of the wonderful tolerance of Hinduism and its desire to embrace other faiths in its pervading atmosphere, that Hindu girls can share outwardly in Christian worship without apparent realization of its incompatability with their ancestral religion. The daily instruction is given in class groups, and where the non-Christian element enters largely there is usually a separate classification for this. Its bearing is stated in simple direct terms by a teacher. "The education of any child is not complete which has not led it consciously to realize the supernatural, and the revelation of God in Christ." In the few schools where a "conscience clause" exists, it is not as a rule taken advantage of. The girls in one convent who were thus exempted sat in the back row quietly and were not asked questions; they also attended chapel, but might take their own books with them. Another curious instance of the working of the Hindu mind is seen in the case of an Indian gentleman who withdrew his daughters from the regular school lesson by virtue of the conscience clause, but sent them back voluntarily to a special Scripture class held once a week. Caste prejudice was possibly justified by this arrangement. The tone and influence of the Christian schools is greatly appreciated; it is this which fills the Diocesan School in Calcutta with pupils, although a thorough education is available in the Bethune School. A high-caste Brahman lady in Bombay testified in the warmest tones to the wonderful character and spirit of the Catholic sisters who had educated her, and to whom she had sent her daughters. It is not only the English education which attracts, it is something more. It would be invidious to multiply instances, but the testimony is practically universal to the acceptability of educational work done in the name of Christ.

The three factors contributing to the education of women in India have thus a varying contribution to make to the most fundamental element in education, and it is this diversity which supplies the keynote to the whole problem, and indicates the line for Western action in the future. The share of the Government, as indicated by the present policy in Eastern Bengal, Madras,[10] the United Provinces, and elsewhere will of necessity become an increasing one in the direct establishment of schools, if there is not a sufficient development of aided schools to meet the rising tide. Its contribution to religion will be a negative one. The spontaneous Indian schools which attempt to supply the need are at their best—and they are not always at their best—only an imperfect solution. It would be but a poor form of Christianity which failed to recognize the diverse manners in which God has revealed Himself to the world, and the truth of permanent value in the great ethnic faiths of the world which finds its final interpretation in That which

[10] *Unrest and Education in India.* Wm. Miller, D.D., LL.D., C.I.E.

is Perfect. There is nothing more striking in the modern reform movements of India than the reflection in them of Christian thought and idealism, and this is specially seen in the instruction given in the girls' schools. Christian hymns are used with certain specific verses left out, the Lord's Prayer is printed in a Parsi manual of devotion, verses from Watts and Charles Kingsley are in the Benares series, and the hope of Christ as the Lode Star of Indian thought can be read in many a school manual. Together with all this is the perpetual allegorizing of such facts in Indian literature as will not bear the pure ethical light. Principal Paranjpe of the Fergusson College at Poona, in arguing at the Bombay Educational Conference for a secular basis for moral teaching, held that to make morality depend upon religion is dangerous if the religious sanction comes to be no longer regarded as binding. His speech is so illuminating as to be worth while quoting in full:—"In times like ours where landmarks that were but yesterday regarded as perennial are being removed to-day and are likely to be forgotten to-morrow, it is best not to cling to too many rocks. The one solid rock on which we can rest is our own reason. If eating pork is a heinous sin with one set of people, beef with another, and any meat at all with a third, how can the alleged basis of morality be regarded as absolute! Especially when, as in India, there are various religions, each religion divided into innumerable sects, and each sect divided into many separate sections; when the feeling aroused by any religious question is of a pitch which can hardly be conceived in Western countries; when the respectability of a man is in inverse ratio to the number of people he is able to associate with without coming into conflict with the prevailing religious ideas—it will be seen that the less we have to do with religion in moulding the character of young children the better for our national being. Let boys be taught to see that there are some principles which they can all believe irrespective of the fact that they belong to one religion or several. It is only in this way that our various races can be brought closer together."[11] To bring morality into relation with a religion which is ethical to the core, and which has attained with modern science and historical criticism only a fuller and deeper content, is to place it on a new footing and to endow it with spiritual power. While full sympathy must be extended to the Indian effort, the emphasis must fall on the Christian schools. They alone can supply in full the religious element so needed in Indian education. The present situation offers to them in increasing measure an opportunity for a voluntary contribution of the needed spiritual force and power to the educational development of India. Their contribution, as already indicated, has been great, but modern conditions demand something more. Old schools must be remodelled, new schools started; independent work must be done

[11] *Allahabad Conference Report*, 1911.

in adapting curricula to Indian ideas and the special needs of girls; the whole educational machinery must be raised to the level of the standard required for men if the opportunity for imparting this spiritual power is to be retained.

No social or religious problem can bear isolation, and if this book has treated the question of the education of women in detail and in its technical bearings, the relation of that question to the Christianizing of Indian life and thought is the main interest in its composition. The problem is a question of character, but of character built upon personal contact with the Christ-life in God—a question of environment and curricula, but also of showing that Christianity is of the East, and Eastern in its spiritual appeal; a question of womanhood, but also of that more perfect human fellowship where Christ is all and in all. "Jesus Christ, by the silent action of a lifetime, laid the first emphasis on the identity of woman's humanity rather than on the difference of her sex, thus both dignifying her and man in his attitude to her."[12] The solution of India's social problem lies in the fulfilment of the Christian ideal, and the progress towards it must be a united one, in which both sexes share alike. The negative influence of the home is often found to be the strongest in the student life of the great Christian colleges, and many an earnest man has fallen back from what he seemed to have gained because of a silent, unseen woman. The work of

[12] *International Review of Missions*, January 1912. Article by T. Gairdner.

Christian education in leavening thought and producing the atmosphere in which there is hope of the ultimate acceptance of Christianity is regarded by many as the most potent influence for the Kingdom of God in India. The great majority of converts in later life, who belonged to the high castes, have been drawn from the ranks of those who have been educated in Christian schools, and in spite of intense opposition there are actually men to-day who seek for baptism during their college career.[13] There is the further, and perhaps in the sure Providence of God the greater, result in the permeation of Hindu society by Christian thought and sentiment, which may yet pave the way for a movement of the higher castes to Christ. At the recent anniversary services of the Prārthanā Samāj in Bombay, the sermon preached by a Justice of the High Court, on the present day as "The Age of the Holy Spirit, the Age of Education," throbbed throughout with the reverence of one who had studied at the feet of Jesus. The long open hall was packed from end to end with young men who had been touched by the new ideas; in one corner sat some twelve Indian women whose sympathies were with them. The disparity of the two sexes in the audience indicated how the leavening influence of Christian education will be deprived of half its power unless it touches the family as the unit of civilization. The "direct result"

[13] The Aim of Educational Missions. *East and West*, January 1912. W. E. S. Holland.

longed for by those who teach in Christian schools is not lacking. It is unnecessary in these days to contradict once more the impression that the baptism of children and girls of immature age is attempted. There are some cases of the baptism of mother and child together, where careful zenana visiting has followed up the school pupil; others—and these are the majority—are secret disciples whose whole environment is massed up against an open confession. One Moslem girl in the higher classes of a Christian school is convinced of the truth of Christianity; every vacation her parents inquire whether she is a Christian yet, and she knows that if she replies in the affirmative all the advantages which her younger sisters are enjoying in another Christian school will cease. The case is not an extreme one. There is a different story of a girl in Burma who was found teaching the children of her jungle village daily, and gathering them on Sundays for Bible stories and hymns, "until," as she put it, "some one comes who can do it better than I." Her former school knew nothing of it, and but for the chance visit of a Commissioner's wife the tale would never have been told. Surely this is direct result.

Christian educational work has also its place in the problem of the Indian Church. Ultimately the interpretation of Christ to India must be through the Indian, and the building up of a strong Indian Christian community is strategically necessary. The power of the Indian Christian home is in proportion to the power of the woman. Yet only 43% of the Christian community are being educated. The dangers of mass movements and of illiterate, uninstructed Christianity on one side, of europeanizing the convert and educating him beyond his capacity on the other, show at the same time the necessity and the difficulty of action. The less romantic educational work of industrial orphanages has its place in the building up of a strong, true community. The training of Christian girls as teachers, through whom the leavening process will again work on the non-Christian village life, is perhaps the most definite and most direct form of influence.

There is no more subtle problem than the lack of any characteristically Indian note in the Indian Christianity which is now assuming some numerical importance. "There is no doubt that the lack of vitality, the half dead and half alive spirituality which is the present characteristic of the Indian Church, is due to enforced conformity to Western standards of what is Christian and what is not Christian."[14] It may be that this problem too has its relation to the education on Christian and Oriental lines of the women, who have been from all time the custodians of religion, the upholders of traditional custom, and conservative rite.[15]

From whatever point the larger question of the whole country is viewed, it seems to attain perspective and reality in relation to the education of its womanhood, and it is only thus as part of one great Christian movement that the feminist problem receives its right emphasis and value.

[14] *Student Movement*, 1911, Article by S. K. Rudra.
[15] Cp. on this *The Renaissance in India*, C. F. Andrews.

XI

CONCLUSION

" Till we all come in the unity of the faith, and of the knowledge of the Son of God, unto a perfect man, unto the measure of the stature of the fulness of Christ."

EPHESIANS iv. 13.

THE spiritual heritage of the twentieth century is marked by extreme diversity and yet by a deep inward reality. The march of science and commerce, and the development of international relationships have given a new content and width to the world's thought. Isolated life is powerless, and a larger synthesis links the human race together. All such relationship must inevitably have spiritual content. The social upheaval, the claim of the individual for recognition, have a determining influence on the interpretation of our faith. Pragmatism in modern philosophy tests religion by its results. The religious evolution necessitated by the play of international forces is all the more critical in that it is to a certain extent unconscious. There is a deep Christianity apart from the Church as it is, which has yet to make the Church its own. The demand is now for reality—an embodiment of religious principles in modern social conditions; for charity—a sympathy with the ethnic faiths which is the surer for belief in the finality of the Christian revelation; for unity, since the modern mind cannot accept a Christianity which does not transcend and interpret all political, social, and intellectual life. "It is not our duty to-day to fight for a new religion; we have but to awaken into freshness of life the fathomless depths of Christianity. In so far as we succeed in doing this, we can completely satisfy the requirements of the new situation; we can seek to realize a Christianity that shall be at once more universal and more active and intent on disengaging itself from its anthropomorphisms; at the same time we shall view as our very own the wealth of religious profundity and inward experience which the older Christianity has gathered through its centuries of service, and shall seek to realize them in our own life." [1]

The growth of the desire to make Christianity universal is perhaps the most wonderful phase in the advance of thought; while in one sense it is very old and a return to the primitive times of the faith, its modern phase thrills with fresh content by the ever-present working of the Spirit of God. The fresh light which criticism has shed on the historical Jesus has thrown once more into relief His wonderful doctrine of the brotherhood of men in the Fatherhood of God. The desire is not so much to bring salvation to those whom a rigid theology long condemned as "heathen," as to give freely of the fulness received in clear

[1] *Christianity and the New Idealism*, Rudolf Eucken.

consciousness of the solidarity of the human race. The world's best thought must be in terms of Christian philosophy; the Kingdom is conceived as present now in power; Christ is seen as the Fulfiller of all that is true and eternal in the ancient Faiths, and essentially the Saviour of the corporate life.

The appeal of this book is thus for the Christianizing of every factor in the education of women in India. None of the three contributing forces need be alien to the Spirit of Christ; their unity, their mutual relationship, and the necessity of their presence in a transitional period must be felt and realized. Can all this educational advance be made, if not directly in the Name of Christ, at least in the power of His Spirit? The Government influence must determine the tone and character of the whole frame-work. Can the Educational Service be supplied in all its branches with women who, while absolutely loyal to the great principle of neutrality, yet seek through it the spiritual in the material, and whose whole work in Empire-building is consciously related to the Kingdom of Christ? India has known men of this type in the Government Service, and has esteemed their strict neutrality the more because of the Christian conviction which lay behind it. The influence of Christian ethics in the Government schools behind such moral instruction as is possible is enormous, and it naturally enters into the teaching of secular subjects. The direct influence permitted out of school hours is a matter of great difficulty and calls for the utmost discretion. If the Government policy were ultimately modified so as to permit of parallel religious instruction, the direct opportunity would be present, but in the meantime indirect religious influence has a very definite place.

The spontaneous Indian element will have an important contribution to make in the determining of the curricula. Will the Indian commimittees, who need the help of English women, be able to secure those of the highest talent and educational qualifications, who for the sake of Christ will give them of their best and remain, if silent, yet strong in the Faith ? This is hard and perplexing work, and calls for strong personalities, but it is fraught with endless possibility. India will never be won if she does not behold Christianity in her midst lived in the lives of those who pursue their ordinary vocation in the Spirit of the Master.

These suggestions are made with hesitation lest their attraction should weigh with those who could take the more definite line of associating themselves with the educational work in India which is done directly in the name of Christ. The development of this work on sound lines by women of experience and of the highest educational qualifications is, as has been indicated in the preceding chapter, the keynote to the whole problem. In no work is there such a magnificent sphere of influence as in this. A spiritual heritage involves responsibility and opportunity. Nearly a century of patient work for the women of India is written in the annals of the Church : the task of the present day is to enter into this work with the same earnest patience. The need for action is urgent. It is not only that there are endless opportunities for new work which are not being utilized, but that schools with an excellent tradition are not being raised to the modern standard of efficiency. They are inevitably handicapped by shortage in the English staff. A young girl of little experience may find herself almost at once at the head of some most complex institution, long before she would ever have had such a position of responsiblity at home. The perpetual strain on those who work on at such tension prevents the due result. In other cases the needed and desired expansion is checked by lack of the trained educator who could supervise village schools and their teachers, or who could put her energy and talent into building up a first-class school for non-Christian girls in the centre of some district where the new spirit is manifest. Facts indicate the appointment in the future of women to act as Tutors or Directresses of Studies to the girl students in the mixed mission colleges. There is the possibility also of women's Christian colleges. On every side the need is apparent, and the power to meet it lies with the women of the English-speaking countries. It is work which makes demands on intellect, on character, and on the religious nature. The hesitation to respond to it springs in part from the sense of reverence for things sacred. There are women in educational circles at home who hold the truth of Christianity and its sufficiency to meet the need of the whole world, but have not offered to share in educational missions lest their contribution be not of the required type. There is need in India for every type of worker. Christianity gains there, as at home, by interpretation through diverse personalities, and there is room for all who can reflect, it may be silently, its spirit and power in the daily routine of work. A sense of vocation is a sense of personal relationship to Him Who calls, and therein lies the motive power for all educational work done in the name of Christ.

Appendix A

Curricula

Matriculation subjects of the five Universities of Calcutta, Madras, Bombay, Panjāb, and Allahabad:—

English and Mathematics, compulsory in all.

History and Geography, compulsory in all except Calcutta.

Science, compulsory in Madras and Bombay; elective in the other three.

Classical language, compulsory in Calcutta, Bombay, Panjāb; alternative with vernacular in Madras; elective in Allahabad.

Vernacular compulsory in Calcutta and Bombay; alternative with classical in Madras; elective in Allahabad and Panjāb.

Drawing, elective in Allahabad and Panjāb.

Text-Books

State Schools.—No choice.

Aided Schools.—Choice among authorized alternatives.

Unaided but recognized Schools.—Abstention from books disapproved by Government.

Text-book Committees.—In every case appointed by Government, and include official and non-official members; in some provinces places are reserved for members of the staff of mission schools.

From Analysis of Educational Codes in British India.

Appendix B

Courses for the Training of Teachers

Training colleges and classes:—

(1) Graduate Course—one year. } Both in English.
(2) Undergraduate Course—two years. }
(3) Vernacular Course—after Middle examination —two years.
(4) Lower Vernacular Course—after Upper Primary examination (women only)—two years.

Courses (1) and (2) are pursued in the Universities, in special English Training schools for men, or in the Training Department of some European schools.

Courses (3) and (4) in Government or mission Vernacular Training schools for women. These consist frequently of very small groups in an ordinary Middle or High school. A few students are also found in mixed schools.

Appendix C

Diagram showing INCREASE OF FEMALE EDUCATION in India.

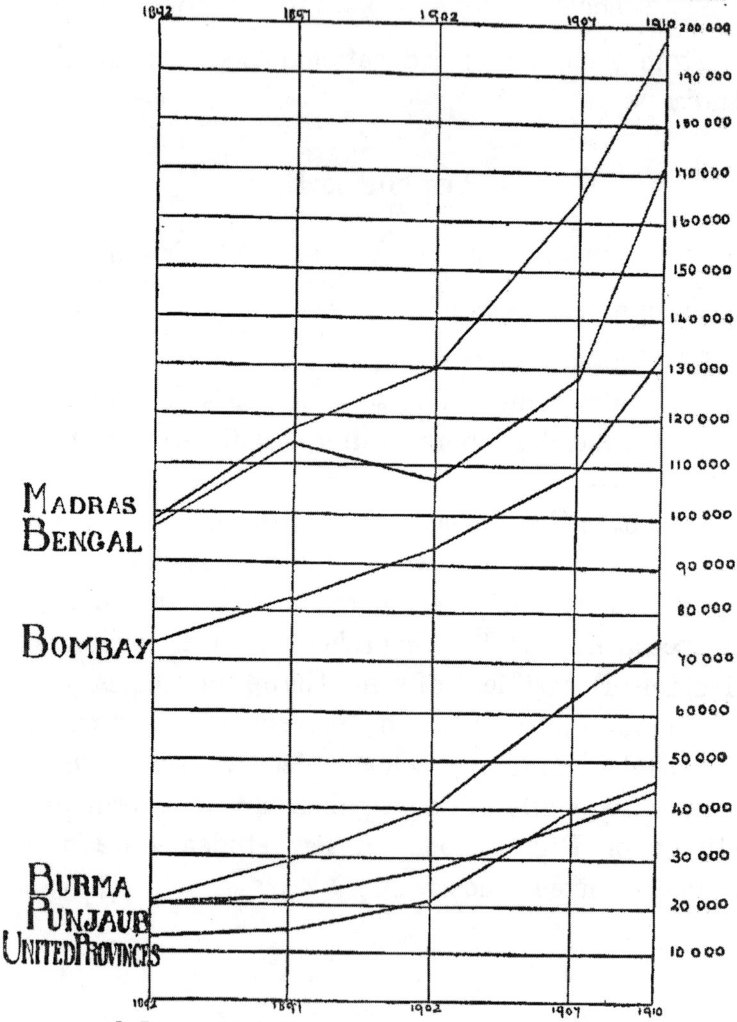

In Burma 9.6% of girls of school age are receiving education.
,, Bombay 7.2% ,, ,, ,, ,,
,, Madras 6.8% ,, ,, ,, ,,
,, Bengal 4.3% ,, ,, ,, ,,
,, Panjāb 3.1% ,, ,, ,, ,,
,, United Provinces 1.3% ,, ,, ,,

Bibliography

BARODA, Maharani of. *Position of Women in Indian Life.*
BRADLEY BIRT, F. B. *Romance of an Eastern Capital.*
CARPENTER, J. E. *Life of Mary Carpenter.*
CARPENTER, M. *Six Months in India.*
CHAILLEY, J. *Administrative Problems in British India.*
CHIROL, Sir VALENTINE. *Indian Unrest.*
DAVIES, E. *Questions relating to Women.*
DUTT, R. C. *Ancient India.*
DUTT, R. C. Translation of *Ramāyana and Mahabhārata.*
FESTINÉ, G. *From the Land of the Princes.*
FRASER, Sir ANDREW. *Among Rajahs and Ryots.*
JAMES, H. R. *Education and Statesmanship in India,* 1797–1910.
LOW, SIDNEY. *A Vision of India.*
LYALL, Sir ALFRED. *Asiatic Studies.*
MITRA, S. C. *Indian Problems.*
NEVINSON, H. W. *The New Spirit in India.*
PURSER, W. C. B. *Christian Missions in Burma.*
POOLE, F. F. *Woman's Influence in the East.*
RICE, B. L. *Mysore.*
RULERS OF INDIA SERIES. Edited by Sir William Hunter.
RICHTER, J. *History of Missions in India.*
SCOTT, Sir GEO. *Burma.*
SMITH, GEO. *Life of Alexander Duff.*
SORABJI, C. *Between the Twilights.*
STEELE, F. A. *India through the Ages.*
STRACHEY, Sir JOHN. *India.*
ZIMMERN, ALICE. *Renaissance of Girls' Education.*

Imperial Gazetteer of India.
Quinquennial Report on Progress of Education in India, 1907.
Public Instruction Reports, 1860–1910. Selections
Statistical Abstract relating to British India, 1911.
Reports of Various Missionary Societies.

Index